Using Technology Evaluation to Enhance Student Learning

Using Technology Evaluation to Enhance Student Learning

Barbara Means

Geneva D. Haertel

EDITORS

Foreword by Linda G. Roberts

Teachers College, Columbia University
New York and London

Published by Teachers College Press, 1234 Amsterdam Avenue, New York, NY 10027

Library of Congress Cataloging-in-Publication Data

Using technology evaluation to enhance student learning / Barbara Means, Geneva D. Haertel, editors; foreword by Linda G. Roberts.
   p.cm.
  Includes bibliographical references and index.
  ISBN 0-8077-4338-0 (pbk.: alk. paper)
   1. Educational technology—Evaluation. 2. Computer-assisted instruction—Evaluation. I. Means, Barbara 1949– II. Haertel, Geneva D.

LB1028.3.U8474 2004
371.33—dc22   2003049341

ISBN 0-8077-4338-0 (paper)

Printed on acid-free paper

Manufactured in the United States of America
11 10 09 08 07 06 05 04   8 7 6 5 4 3 2 1

Contents

Foreword

Dramatic advances in computer and telecommunications technology have occurred over the past decade. These advances have lowered the cost of technology while increasing capabilities for applications that cut across society, including education. If we were to draw a map of the "technology horizon," we would see tremendous forces shaping the future of teaching and learning (Grove Consultants International and Institute for the Future, 2000), including massive amounts of information accessible via the Internet, smarter appliances, and devices that are becoming increasingly interconnected, miles of fiber that are bringing high-speed access to more and more schools, homes, and communities, and users who are inventing applications never dreamed of by the designers.

Since 1995, local communities, states, and the federal government invested heavily in technology for the nation's schools and classrooms. This first national technology plan challenged America's schools to reach four goals: training for teachers, computers for students, classrooms connected to the Internet, and development of effective software and on-line learning resources. (U.S. Department of Education, Office of Educational Technology, 1996.) Today virtually all our public K–12 schools and almost three out of four classrooms connect to the Internet. The student-to-computer ratio has improved to a national average of five students per computer. In a small number of schools every student has a computer. Increasing numbers of new teachers are coming to the classroom with preparation to use these twenty-first-century tools, and they join colleagues who are also gaining skill and confidence in using technology across the curriculum (U.S. Department of Education, Office of Educational Technology, 2001). But what is missing?

The prevailing view that schools are slow to embrace change notwithstanding, much of the investment in technology has been driven by schools' willingness to experiment and innovate. Parents believe that their children should know how to use modern technology and become technologically literate, and schools have responded to this demand. Increasingly, however, educators and government officials (from Congress to local school boards) believe that it's time for schools to demonstrate the value of the technology infrastructure. They want to see evidence of effectiveness before they invest further in more computers, more teacher training, and expanded telecommunications capacity.

As Director of the Office of Educational Technology, I listened as the calls for research intensified. In March 1997 the report of the Panel on Educational Technology of the President's Committee of Advisors on Science and Technology (PCAST) called for a large-scale program of rigorous, systematic research. Many other reports and policymakers echoed these recommendations. In response, the U.S. Department of Education required Technology Innovation Grant projects to build evaluation into their 5-year demonstration programs and partnerships. Similarly, states and districts began to conduct their own studies of educational technology, including some that encompassed a large number of students and classrooms. A number of these studies have helped identify applications and strategies that work. The Interagency Education Research Initiative was established with the goal of building on prior work, identifying technology-supported innovations that had some evidence of effectiveness and funding investigations of their effectiveness on a broader scale. (This initiative is supported by the National Science Foundation, U.S. Department of Education, and the National Institutes of Health.)

Nevertheless, I was still convinced that we could do better. Most studies of technology's impact on students looked only at short-term effects and were either small in scale (e.g., a few selected classrooms or schools) or lacking in detailed information about just what technology-supported learning experiences students had had. I believed that researchers could improve the design and collection of data. Just as new technology created new opportunities for learning, it created ways to invent new tools for research and evaluation, particularly ways to track and monitor what, how, and when learning occurred. The question for me was how to move forward in a practical way? A compelling strategy emerged at a high-level seminar on technology and education held by the U.S. Department of Education and the Brazil Ministry of Education, hosted at SRI International headquarters in Menlo Park, California, on December 2–3, 1998. The meeting was the Second U.S.–Brazil Binational Dialogue on Education, an activity of the U.S.–Brazil Partnership for Education launched in Brasilia on October 14, 1997, with the support of Presidents Clinton and Cardozo.

Participants heard again that many studies pointed to the promising impacts of technology, but also learned that in all too many cases there were more questions than answers. Classroom access to technology was expanding. All across the country, there were districts that could be rich sources of data and schools that could be laboratories for the development of the next generation of interactive learning resources. Certainly, this was the time to invest in research and evaluation: What would it take to conduct a set of rigorous studies? Was there a base of theory to build on? Were the tools for analysis adequate? Was it possible to conduct serious evaluation in classroom settings where change and revision were continuous? Where was it best to begin?

The researchers around the table suggested a compelling strategy for getting started: invite experts in research and evaluation from diverse fields to share their knowledge and experience, and design new studies that could be undertaken. Soon after the U.S.–Brazil Dialogue, SRI submitted a field-initiated proposal to the Office of Educational Technology and the result is the collection of chapters, dialogue, and analysis presented in *Evaluating Educational Technology: Effective Research Designs for Improving Learning* (Haertel & Means, 2003) and this companion volume.

These two volumes provide both theoretical constructs and pragmatic designs that address different uses of technology within different settings for different purposes. A reading of the papers from the experts makes clear that no one study will answer all the critical questions. Furthermore, the process won't be easy, given the many different purposes for which various technologies are used and the complexity of fully integrating technology into teaching and learning. The research and evaluation designs also make clear that it will be essential to develop new assessment tools to tap into the kinds of deep understanding and complex skills that technology-based innovations are trying to foster.

These volumes will be an invaluable resource for the academic community and those who are engaged in the evaluation of projects and initiatives in the United States and in other countries as well. Examples of better assessment will help state and local education decision makers plan new evaluation efforts using measures that are more sensitive than standardized tests at detecting technology's effects. These new assessments not only can provide evidence of technology's effects on knowledge and skills in subject areas, but also can reveal the degree to which students have acquired technological skills that can be used to support their schoolwork and other activities. The volumes also present examples of more rigorous research and evaluation designs that can guide the collection of evidence in order to confirm or refute causal claims about the efficacy of technology in educational settings. Such multivariate designs illustrate the need for studies that attend to the many influences that can moderate technology's effects.

I am hopeful that the challenges to be faced, along with the chance to shape the development of the next generation of technology for learning, will capture the interest and imagination of a new cadre of researchers, those not yet immersed in educational technology but already involved in the study of cognition and learning, and those who have gained their expertise in other related fields.

These volumes are timely. The Elementary and Secondary Education Act of 2001 calls for rigorous evaluations of programs, particularly those funded under Title II, Part D, Technology. Congressional leaders want to see evidence of the impact of the technology programs on student academic achievement, including the technological literacy of all students. The legislation also calls on states and districts to evaluate the effectiveness of their technology efforts, particularly with regard to the integration of technology into curricula and instruction, as well as effectiveness in increasing the ability of teachers to teach, and enabling students to meet challenging state academic content standards. Finally, the new education bill requires the Secretary of Education to conduct an independent, long-term study of educational technology.

There is much to be accomplished. I am confident that this collection of papers and new thinking on the design of rigorous evaluations of technology and learning and on the assessments that can best document their effects will make important contributions to the field: (1) gaining the attention of researchers as well as bringing experts from other disciplines into the field; (2) improving the evaluations of technology-supported innovations; (3) stimulating the development of technology-based data collection tools and analysis; (4) shaping the federal education research agenda; and, most importantly, (5) expanding our theory and knowledge.

The work in *Evaluating Educational Technology* and this companion volume also lends support to policies and practice that focus on the integration of technology into teaching and learning. In the process of asking better questions and improving the tools for analysis, we can enhance our ability to get the most solid contributions to students' learning from our investment in technology.

Linda G. Roberts
Former Director
U.S. Department of Education
Office of Educational Technology

REFERENCES

Grove Consultants International and the Institute for the Future. (2000). *The educational technology horizon map and user guidebook*. San Francisco, CA: Author.

Haertel, G. D., & Means, B. (Eds.). (2003). *Evaluating educational technology: Effective research designs for improving learning*. New York: Teachers College Press.

President's Committee of Advisors on Science and Technology, Panel on Educational Technology. (1997).*Report to the President on the use of technology to strengthen K–12 education in the U.S.* Washington, DC: Author.

U.S. Department of Education, Office of Educational Technology. (1996). *Getting America's students ready for the 21st century: Meeting the technology literacy challenge*. Washington, DC: Author.

U.S. Department of Education, Office of Educational Technology. (2001). *E-learning: Putting world-class education at the fingertips of all children*. Washington, DC: Author.

Introduction

Few research areas in education have been more controversial than studies of the impact of technology on student learning (Oppenheimer, 1997; Stoll, 1995). While technology proponents hold forth a vision of students and teachers participating in technology-supported learning environments featuring individualized instruction, interactive simulations, and tools for knowledge representation and organization, policymakers look for positive effects on large-scale assessments linked to content standards. Some argue that traditional approaches to schooling have resisted any significant reshaping in response to the availability of technology, just as they proved impervious to the influence of television, teaching machines, and radio (Cuban, 2000). Other critics argue that technology does indeed affect schools, but that its impacts are largely negative—diverting resources from more worthy pursuits (such as art, music, or basic skills) and wasting students' and teachers' time with the intellectually trivial mechanisms of technology use.

Public perceptions of technology's role in education have long been influenced by "gee-whiz" articles describing classrooms using new technologies and photo opportunities presented when grade school children explore virtual reality environments or high schoolers program robots for competition. More recently, however, press coverage has included a distinctly skeptical voice concerning the paucity of evidence that technology has produced positive impacts on student learning. Even in the heart of the technology industry in Silicon Valley, a local journalist asserted in a December 2002 edition of the *San Jose Mercury News*, "There still isn't any good evidence that computers significantly improve teaching and learning" (Rodriguez, 2002).

POLICYMAKERS AND PRACTITIONERS AS CONSUMERS AND SPONSORS OF RESEARCH

Given the tremendous stakes involved in creating a technology infrastructure for schools or launching a major technology–based instructional innovation, policymakers, and practitioners would do well to examine the research base on learning technologies both for evidence regarding technology's effects and for insights into what is required to make it successful. Familiarity not only with the pertinent research studies but also with issues surrounding their quality and interpretation can make policymakers and practitioners more informed consumers of educational research. With the increasing emphasis on justifying educational practices on the basis of scientific research found in the latest federal education legislation (the No Child Left Behind Act of 2001), it will be important for consumers of research to weigh contradictory findings using information on each study's design, instrumentation, and analyses. A thoughtful examination of each study's qualities will help identify the best evidence to guide practice.

The involvement of policymakers and practitioners with learning technology research, however, should go beyond that of being intelligent consumers. We believe that they need to be involved in setting the agenda for future research as well.

Reflecting its multiple origins in philosophy, psychology, anthropology, and sociology, educational research and evaluation are characterized by a wide range of research methods and nearly constant controversy over their respective utilities and rigor. Different methods were designed to serve different purposes and to answer different types of questions. Hence many of the debates over the desirability of one method versus another really need to be framed as decisions concerning what questions should have the highest priority in designing the research. In educational research, with its intended purpose of providing knowledge that can be used to improve education, the setting of priorities around research questions should not be left to researchers alone. These are fundamentally issues of policy and practice, and policymakers and practitioners should be partnering in, if not leading, the setting of the research agenda.

This volume is a companion piece to *Evaluating Educational Technology: Effective Research Designs for Improving Learning* (Haertel & Means, 2003), which presents research designs and issues primarily for a research or research-training audience. This volume is intended to serve the needs of educational technology policymakers and practitioners. We believe, however, that this volume can provide insights for those practicing or undergoing training in research and evaluation as well. In this volume, we relate the issues coming out of the research design chapters in the research volume to the concerns and needs of those shaping policy and practice in the educational technology area. Certainly in our own experience, we have found it extremely useful to step back from questions concerning the technical implementation of research to consider the concerns and goals of those who are in a position to do something with findings from our research and evaluation studies.

WHY TECHNOLOGY EVALUATION IS DIFFICULT

Many factors contribute to the complexity and difficulty of evaluating the effects of technology use in schools. One of the most obvious challenges is the sheer number of technologies and technology uses that might be evaluated. It's very simple to use the word *technology,* but what do we include when we try to actually study it? Even if we limit ourselves to computer-based technologies, the number of different technologies finding their way into classrooms is huge. We have computer analogs not just to worksheets, books, encyclopedias, blackboards, and typewriters, but also to drafting boards, three-dimensional models, slide rules, and dissecting tables.

Beyond the sheer number of technologies, there is a deeper layer of complexity in defining what it is that we wish to evaluate. No one believes that merely pulling up to a school building with a truckload of notebook computers is going to improve student learning. Clearly, it is the teaching and learning experiences supported or mediated by technology that will potentially produce the desired effects. What needs to be studied is not the hardware nor even the hardware and software per se, but rather the instructional experience that students receive. Moreover, that instructional experience is likely to vary depending on the teacher's background, teaching philosophy, and training and experience as well as on the characteristics of the students. Research designs need to take these factors into account. It will be difficult to identify students who have exactly the same backgrounds and receive exactly the same instructional experiences as those receiving a technology intervention except for the presence of technology. Pedagogy and content are usually confounded. In many cases, this is intentionally so because learning technology developers set their goal as providing learning experiences that would be impossible without the technology.

One of the requirements for many research designs is keeping a clear distinction between the experimental *treatment* and the experiences of a control group. Depending on the technology use under consideration, the student population, and time frame selected for the study, instituting and maintaining this distinction can be problematic. With common types of technology applications, such as word processing and Internet search engines, it would be unrealistic to expect that the control group members would not experience some variation of the technology provided in the experimental group's classrooms. Moreover, students' prior experience with, expertise in, and home access to technology may be significant factors, as may technology use in classes other than those in which the experiment is being conducted (especially the case when middle school and high school classes are the sample under study).

Finally, the definition and measurement of student learning outcomes is often problematic. In many cases, technology-based interventions seek to foster analytic, problem-solving, or design skills that are not covered by conventional achievement tests. Using an outcome measure that has nothing to do with the intervention under study can easily mask real impacts on learning.

WHY BOTHER EVALUATING EDUCATIONAL TECHNOLOGY?

Given the complexities of the research enterprise alluded to above, one might ask, "Why bother?" Several of the authors providing commentaries in this volume do in fact pose this question. As they point out, technology is getting implemented in schools or classrooms whether or not there is strong research evidence linking technology to improved student achievement. Valerie Lee, in particular, poses the question, "If we're going to use technology in schools anyway, why invest large amounts of money and effort in studies to determine whether or not it's effective?" The question is a good one and requires a reasonable answer if we expect people to read this book.

While some policymakers and communities will choose to invest in technology because they regard it as an essential part of the modern world and something that should be available to the enterprise of education just as it is to business, health care, and entertainment, others are more skeptical. Over the last several years, we have been spending something on the order of $7 billion a year to equip American schools and teachers to incorporate technology in education. Nor is it a one-time cost. Technology is constantly changing, and new software requires increasingly powerful computers. One expects to need to replace a computer inventory every 3 to 5 years. The tremendous investment in computer and network technology that American schools made in the late 1990s is coming up for renewal. States and school districts, facing the budget deficits associated with an economic downturn, are having to ask themselves whether replacing or upgrading their equipment and software is worth the cost. John Bailey (2002), the current director of the Office of Educational Technology within the U.S. Department of Education, believes that without solid research evidence of technology's benefits, states and districts are on the verge of reversing their commitment to technology implementation. *The San Jose Mercury News* writer Joe Rodriguez (2002), quoted earlier regarding the lack of solid evidence of technology's effectiveness, offered this assessment in response to the rhetorical question, "Are you ready for the next technocure for education?" After asserting that there is no "good" evidence, he argues, "Even if anecdotal successes are good enough for some people, they don't justify the enormous costs and cuts in music, art, field trips, science, and other programs that usually happen when computer fever takes hold."

We believe that most schools and districts will continue to work on technology integration. But even if policymakers are unlikely to decide *not* to implement technology in schools, there is still a good reason for conducting research on technology's effects. As a nation, we are making a tremendous investment in technology for schools. We are asking prospective and practicing teachers to learn technology skills and techniques for using technology in their instruction. We are giving our kids time with software and the Internet in an environment where everyone feels there is not enough time for them to learn everything they need to prepare them for further schooling and adulthood. Given the level of spending of precious dollars and hours on technology-based activities, we have an obligation to learn as much as we can about how to do it right. We need to know not just which technology uses make us feel good, but which have real, long-term payoffs for our students and the adults who work with them in schools and how to implement those technologies to maximize benefits.

INSIGHTS POLICYMAKERS AND PRACTITIONERS CAN GAIN

This volume is intended to stimulate deeper and more informed thinking about evaluative research that has been done and needs to be done in the learning technology area. Important insights include:

- *Let the research question drive the choice of method.* The positions most often articulated in the current debate over the place of random-assignment experiments in education research ("only research using this kind of a design is scientific" versus "it's impossible to do experiments in our school system") are simplistic and unnecessarily adversarial. We would do better to work on formulating an understanding of when experimental methods add value and are feasible. In the realm of educational technology research, shorter term, well-defined interventions are the best candidates for experimental evaluation.
- *Look for critical influences at multiple levels of the education system.* Education in America occurs within a system that has multiple levels—the individual student's home and local community, the classroom, the school, the district, and the state. Conditions and actions at each of these levels interact to influence educational experiences and, potentially, learning outcomes. Our conceptual models of how a technology-supported intervention will produce positive outcomes

need to take important factors at each of these levels into account. Both understanding and predicting short- and long-term outcomes will require measurement of key features of the context and the implementation activities within multiple levels of the education system.

- *Figure out what you're trying to teach—and measure that.* Whether or not a technology-based intervention can be demonstrated to enhance student learning will be critically dependent on what are used as learning measures. Many times, the convenience of using assessments that students already have to complete—usually state-mandated achievement tests—and the importance of these measures in district, state, and federal accountability systems will make the use of test scores attractive. There are many cases in which, given the nature of the technology intervention, this choice makes sense. There are many individual technology-based interventions, however, that involve content and skills that are not covered by the standardized tests. This is particularly the case with extended problem-solving and high-order reasoning skills, which are difficult to capture in standard test item formats. When the nature of the intervention and the contents of the assessment don't match, we would not expect to see large positive effects on test scores, and should be suspicious if they are reported.
- *Support the development of more good assessments of student learning.* One of the barriers to rigorous research on learning technology interventions targeting higher order thinking and problem solving is the lack of appropriate learning measures with credibility and the technical qualities needed for statistical analysis. Developing such assessments would be a major undertaking. (Mislevy and his colleagues discuss an approach for doing so in their chapter, "Improving Educational Assessment," in *Evaluating Educational Technology.*)
- *Look for ways to evaluate the long-term costs and benefits of the technology infrastructure.* While controversy rages about whether or not to use experimental designs to evaluate individual technology-based interventions, policymakers and the public seek an answer to a broader question. The implementation of a technology-based intervention requires the presence of a technology infrastructure (wiring, network connection, computers, teacher training). These investments are made not just to support the use of one piece of software to teach a particular topic but to support teaching and learning in multiple subject areas and grades. The medical analogue is not the decision of whether or not to administer Drug A, but rather the decision of whether or not to invest in building a pharmaceutical plant. Understanding and measuring the effects of

providing this infrastructure require following students, teachers, and schools over a period of years, and pose different design challenges than does the evaluation of a discrete technology-based intervention.

ORGANIZATION OF THIS VOLUME

This volume is organized into four parts. Each of the first three parts deals with a theme emerging from two or more of the research design chapters in *Evaluating Educational Technology*. For each of these sections we provide an introduction to the issues related to the theme and summarize the major points of the related research design chapters. These sections do not require readers to have read the research chapters in the research volume; rather they provide the detail necessary to understand the key issues. We then present reactions to the chapters in the form of commentaries written by external reviewers representing either a policy or a research methodology perspective.

Part I addresses the question "What Kind of Learning Technology Research Best Addresses Policymakers' Needs?" Here we deal with the current controversy concerning the status that random-assignment experiments should have in the research and evaluation agenda. Julia Stapleton, a state-level policymaker, and Nick Smith, a professor of education and current President of the American Evaluation Association, respond to the chapters related to this theme.

Part II turns to the issue of how we measure student learning. Jim Pellegrino, a university professor of psychology and researcher who has been active both in the area of assessment and in that of learning technology implementation in schools, provides a commentary.

Part III deals with the problem of trying to evaluate the long-term effects of technology writ large: that is, the impact of an investment in a technology infrastructure at the school or district level. Valerie Lee, a professor and researcher who has examined the effects of many school features other than technology, provides a perspective on the research recommendations in this area.

Part IV of this volume addresses the issue of a research agenda for educational technology directly. After summarizing the funding that federal agencies have made available for learning technology research in the past, we discuss limitations of earlier funding strategies and make recommendations for a four-part program of research. The recommended research areas reflect our interpretation of recommendations made in the chapters in the research volume, but should not be construed as the opinion of any of the other authors. Finally, we close with a commentary by Nora Sabelli, who brings her experience in setting policy around learning technology research at the federal level to the task of providing some perspective on the proposed research agenda.

WHAT KIND OF LEARNING TECHNOLOGY RESEARCH BEST ADDRESSES POLICYMAKERS' NEEDS?

The size of the national investment in bringing technology into our nation's schools has for some time led many policymakers to call for definitive research on the effects of the investment. This position has now become official national policy: The No Child Left Behind Act (NCLB) of 2001 calls for the Secretary of Education to "conduct a rigorous, independent, long-term evaluation of the impact of educational technology on student achievement using scientifically based research methods and control conditions." (See Section 2421a, Part D, of Title II of the enabling legislation.) In Part I we consider both the intention of Congress in framing this requirement, and the perspectives of local and state policymakers and the research community, with respect to what would constitute rigorous and worthwhile research in the field of learning technology.

THE POLICY ENVIRONMENT FOR EDUCATIONAL RESEARCH

The seemingly confusing and contradictory body of research purporting to evaluate the effectiveness of educational technology needs to be considered within the context of educational research more broadly. Educational research has long been characterized by a diversity of methods and intense debates within the research community about their relative merits. Within the policy community, we have seen decades of suspicion on the part of some in Congress that educational research is subject to investigator biases and that the federal agencies funding educational research

9

tend to sponsor investigations sympathetic to their political orientation. More recently, both the legislative and the executive branches of government have expressed concern about the scientific quality of educational research. In arguing for an independent education research academy, Representative Michael Castle (Republican, Delaware), for example, asserted, "Education research is broken in our country...and Congress must work to make it more useful...research needs to be conducted on a more scientific basis" (Viadero, 2000, p. 30).

The latest federal education legislation, the NCLB Act, attempts to fulfill Castle's vision. The legislation not only defines scientifically based research but requires that local education agencies receiving federal compensatory education funding, federal teacher training dollars, or money for technology implementation demonstrate that the approaches and materials they use are backed by "scientifically based research." In all, there are more than 100 references to "scientifically based research" in No Child Left Behind (Olson & Viadero, 2002).

The legislation defines *scientifically based research* as "research that involves the application of rigorous, systematic, and objective procedures to obtain reliable and valid knowledge relevant to education activities and programs," a definition with which few would argue. However, the bill goes on to stipulate that scientifically based research "includes experimental or quasi-experimental designs in which individuals, entities, programs, or activities are assigned to different conditions and with appropriate controls to evaluate the effects of the conditions of interest, with a preference for random-assignment experiments, or other designs to the extent that those designs contain within-condition or across-condition controls." (An earlier version of the bill defined scientific research in education as *only* experiments with random assignment.) Specific wording aside, most in both the policy and the research communities have come to interpret the legislation's use of the phrase "scientifically based research" as code for random-assignment experiments.

This movement has been further promulgated by the U.S. Department of Education, which announced that it would be taking a new approach to program evaluation. "Even with high-quality fast-response surveys, annual performance data, and descriptive studies, we still cannot answer the question on the minds of practitioners: 'What works?' To be able to make causal links between interventions and outcomes, we need rigorous field trials, complete with random assignment, value-added analysis of longitudinal achievement data, and distinct interventions to study" (U.S. Department of Education, 2002).

This perspective is reflected in the Department of Education's implementation of a congressionally mandated longitudinal study of educational technology. In calling for the development of a design for this study, the department has stipulated that the study be not only longitudinal in design but also incorporate random assignment.

Not surprisingly, many in the education research community are uneasy about legislators dealing with issues of research methodology (Berliner, 2002; Olson & Viadero, 2002). Beyond the fact that members of a profession resent outside direction with respect to their practice, the prevailing policy climate is sparking numerous debates concerning the desirability, feasibility, and relevance of random-assignment experiments within education research (Erickson & Gutierrez, 2002; Feuer, Towne, & Shavelson, 2002).

While the chapters in *Evaluating Educational Technology* were commissioned prior to the NCLB act and the implementation of more rigorous methodologies in the Department of Education evaluations, they do reflect the same divergent methodological perspectives, which are vying for dominance within the education research community today. In this section, we consider these alternative perspectives and their claims both for methodological rigor and for policy relevance.

Tom Cook and Lincoln Moses are strong proponents of random-assignment experiments. Alan Lesgold, Katie Culp and her colleagues, and Eva Baker and Joan Herman argue for the use of other methods that they believe are better suited to the study of the *context* within which an educational application of technology is implemented and how context influences the technology's effects.

WHAT IS A TRUE EXPERIMENT?

The distinguishing feature of a "true" or random-assignment experiment is that the treatment that an individual (or class or school) receives is determined by the experimenter—and not by the individual's (or class's or school's) preference or bureaucratic convenience. This stipulation is essential because it is the only way we can be sure that there is not some other characteristic (such as involved parents, effective teachers, or intelligent students) differentially associated with the decision to implement or not implement the intervention under study. (Designs in which there is a control group intended to match the group receiving the experimental treatment as well as possible, but where group membership is not assigned by the experimenter, are called *quasi-experimental*. These designs are open to the criticism that there may always be some characteristic on which the two groups were not matched that has influenced outcomes.)

The necessary components of a random-assignment experiment are articulated in more detail by Moses (2000):

- The treatments being compared are actively imposed on the experimental units, in contrast to the observation of treatments or innovations where they happen to occur.
- All treatments (or the experimental treatment and the control or no-treatment condition) are applied within the same time period.
- After a group of eligible study subjects is defined, each receives one of the treatments or is assigned to the control condition by random choice.
- The whole enterprise is organized and conducted in accordance with a written experimental protocol.
- After random assignment, all measures and processes other than the treatment under test that may affect the data are symmetrically applied to all study subjects.
- The unit of treatment application and randomization (whether students, classes, schools, or districts) is the unit of a statistical analysis and defines the sample size.

Application of this experimental method can be used to ascertain whether an individual treatment is effective ("what works," in policy jargon) or which of several alternative treatments is most effective. Experimentalists often argue for their approach through analogies to research in medicine. In both medicine and education, they argue, the field considers a treatment that is intended to produce a beneficial effect. While recognizing that the world is a messy place, experimentalists point to the random-assignment experiment as the best method yet devised to rise above that messiness and establish a causal relationship between Treatment A and Effect B.

THE CASE FOR RANDOMIZED EXPERIMENTS IN EDUCATIONAL TECHNOLOGY RESEARCH

In the research volume, Thomas D. Cook of Northwestern University, a well-known advocate of the use of random-assignment experiments in education, teamed up with researchers Barbara Means, Geneva D. Haertel, and Vera Michalchik from SRI International's Center for Technology in Learning to explore how an experimental design could be applied in evaluating the effectiveness of a common use of technology in schools today. In their chapter, "The Case for Randomized Experiments," the authors pose a thought experiment—how could an experiment be designed to answer the question "What effect does doing Internet research have on student learning?"

The authors discuss the need to outline the processes that in theory link the particulars of the intervention to desired outcomes. In this case, the nature of the students' research topic and the instruction or coaching students receive on how to do research are factors likely to affect what students learn. The experience of conducting research on the Internet could be hypothesized to enhance a variety of student outcomes, including engagement with intellectual content, inquiry and communication skills, knowledge of the subject matter content, and technology skills. The need to measure content knowledge and the desirability of having a common treatment (or *experimental protocol*) suggest the wisdom of confining the experiment to a specific content area and grade level. The authors chose 11th-grade American history for their example.

Cook et al. recognize that schools or classrooms assigned to a particular condition may not implement it as intended. They discuss the importance of measuring what actually does get implemented in individual classrooms. Similarly, other factors that might mediate the relationship between Internet searches and student learning—for example, the computer infrastructure, teacher's familiarity with Internet information sources and search techniques, and so on—should be documented. They also discuss the issue of obtaining cooperation from participating schools and classrooms and the need to provide incentives in order to increase the representativeness of the schools and teachers willing to participate.

Having sketched out a possible experimental study, the authors then discuss the objections that some members of the educational evaluation community have raised against doing experiments. They assert that the objection that experiments use an oversimplified model of causation does not prevent critics from taking action based on simple, assumed causal relations (such as "time on task increases learning"). A related objection is incompatibility of experiments with the complex organizations and highly localized policies and practices within educational systems. Some educators argue that the causal knowledge produced by experiments obscures each school's uniqueness and oversimplifies the multivariate and nonlinear ways in which politics and social relationships structure educational reform. While not denying this complexity, the authors point out the commonality of purposes, roles, and issues in America's schools. Moreover, they assert that diversity calls for larger sample sizes, not for abandoning the design that can best isolate causal relationships within complex systems. (See the contrasting treatment of this issue by Culp et al. described later.) Acknowledging critics' arguments that experimental findings are limited in their generalizability because of limitations in the range of schools willing to participate and the great variation in school contexts, Cook et al. nevertheless assert,

"Until a causal claim is established, it makes little sense to ask about its generalization."

After addressing objections to the use of experiments in educational settings, the authors describe an alternative to the experiment that has been widely used in the educational technology field—the *design experiment*. (This is not the technical use of the term *experiment* as research design specialists would use it.) Design experiments, which are predominant in disciplines such as architecture, engineering, and software development, involve working with practitioners to implement the kinds of practices the researcher wants to study. Design experiments in classrooms implementing new learning technologies involve helping to implement those technologies as well as documenting what happens when they are introduced and as various modifications are tried out. Design experiments lack the researcher control and prespecification of treatments used by true experiments, but they share a commitment to an open-minded approach to problem solving. Design experiments are valued by developers and consumers for their contributions to improving technology implementation designs. Most evaluators, on the other hand, reject this approach as a strategy for establishing the effectiveness of an intervention.

Cook et al. conclude with a discussion of randomized experiments as the "gold standard" in addressing causal effects. They argue that while, in theory, the experiment is the method of choice for establishing causal claims, a more modest case has to be made for the use of random assignment in school practice due to the complexities of classroom and school settings. However, there is no alternative that has the same power to test whether a particular treatment produces a specified outcome. They argue that the objections raised to experimental designs can be handled through design enhancements such as participation incentives, adequate sample sizes, and documentation of implementation processes.

ALTERNATIVES TO THE EXPERIMENTAL APPROACH

Not all education researchers are swayed by the experimentalists' arguments. Critics point out that the experimental method's ability to determine that A causes B in the settings in which the experiment is conducted does not (1) lead to an understanding of *why* A causes B or (2) reveal the range of conditions under which A would cause B. These researchers argue that one needs to understand why A causes B in order to know what variants of A would also be likely to work. Equally important is the related issue of understanding the range of conditions under which A causes B. Failure of programs that work in one setting to be efficacious in another is well documented within education (Berliner, 2002; Cronbach & Snow, 1977). Moreover, technology itself is changing at a rapid pace.

Experimental evaluations of technology's impact would be highly susceptible to what Berliner (2002) calls "decade by findings interactions." Findings obtained in research during one decade may no longer hold 10 years later, not because the original research was flawed but simply because there have been real changes in social systems. To this we would add, in the case of technology, real changes in the treatment. Comparing the cumbersome file transfer mechanisms available in 1990 to the Web resources and Internet search engines available in 2000 illustrates the point. Ironically, reviews of studies performed on what would be considered very primitive basic skills practice programs in the 1980s are still cited today as justification for purchasing educational software with little resemblance to the programs used in the research. By the time the kind of randomized, longitudinal experiment on educational technology that the U.S. Department of Education recently has called for is brought to a close, there is the risk that the technology used in the experiment would be considered obsolete.

The way in which learning technology—or any educational intervention—gets implemented will depend on a wide range of contextual factors, including the belief system and experience of the teachers putting the program into place, the technology infrastructure and availability of technical support when problems occur, the students and their prior achievement and technology skills, and so on. Experiments that demonstrate overall or "main" effects can be misleading, in these researchers' view, because those effects are in fact averages generally based on large positive effects in some circumstances and negligible or even negative effects in others. They seek to understand the conditions necessary for obtaining a positive effect. While experimentalists, such as Tom Cook, view such questions as appropriate once a positive main effect has been established, researchers emphasizing context see limited value in demonstrating an average effect if we cannot predict for any particular local circumstance whether or not the same positive outcome would be likely to be obtained.

Many of these researchers regard the implementation of technology in schools as a forgone conclusion. They believe that in the "trenches" where decisions about local programs are made, policymakers need research that will help them predict whether an intervention will work in their local circumstance and understand what they need to do to enhance the likelihood of success. Thus, instead of "What works?" the question these researchers ponder is "What works *when?*"

DETERMINING THE EFFECTS OF TECHNOLOGY IN COMPLEX SCHOOL ENVIRONMENTS

In his chapter in *Evaluating Educational Technology*, "Detecting Technology's Effects in Complex School Environments," Alan Lesgold of the University of Pittsburgh notes that a random-assignment experiment has the potential to detect the effects of a single factor of interest if that factor alone is sufficient to produce the desired effect. But, according to Lesgold, in education this is rarely so: Success usually comes from a cluster of causes, and this is particularly true in the case of technology. In fact, Lesgold argues, technology is generally not a direct cause of change but rather a *facilitator* or amplifier of various educational practices. Before doing a costly experiment, in Lesgold's view, we need to develop and, to the extent possible, validate a causal model incorporating the full range of factors that might influence the outcomes of interest. Lesgold argues that a full range of data and analysis, including case studies and detailed descriptive studies, will assist policymakers by helping to convey the nature of the contextual features that will influence the success of a given educational intervention.

Lesgold uses causal modeling to illustrate how a researcher might determine the contexts and specific conditions in which a particular technology innovation works. Components within Lesgold's model include teacher and student inputs, prior infrastructure for information processing tool usage, professional development context, technology enhancement implementation, and teacher and student outcomes.

Lesgold asserts, "If the essential evaluation question is 'what works when,' then it is essential to develop a standard means of specifying the *when* part of this formulation." As part of his approach to specifying context (the "when"), Lesgold sets forth the idea of *maturity models*. A maturity model contains (1) a set of features on which students, classrooms, or schools can vary; (2) a set of stages of maturity; and (3) for each feature, a scoring rubric for deciding how mature the student, classroom, or school is on that feature.

Four types of maturity that Lesgold believes are likely to be related to the effectiveness of a technology innovation are instructional maturity, technology infrastructure maturity, educational software product maturity, and people maturity. The success of an innovation often may depend on the maturity of the context in which it is implemented. Various aspects of maturity (e.g., instructional processes, software maturity) interact, with one kind of maturity potentiating increased maturity of other forms (e.g., maturity of the software may increase instructional maturity).

Lesgold concludes his chapter by addressing four broad research strategies and their feasibility for use in generating information on technology use and effects. The strategies he considers include studies of the necessary preconditions for an intervention, descriptive studies of intervention implementation, cost-benefit analyses, and randomized field studies. Lesgold recommends the use of longitudinal test beds that can be used initially to collect context data on technology implementations and eventually as the location for "microstudies" that provide data on specific innovations.

LINKING EVALUATION TO SCHOOL IMPROVEMENT

In their chapter, "Achieving Local Relevance and Broader Influence," Katherine McMillan Culp, Margaret Honey, and Robert Spielvogel of the Center for Children and Technology emphasize the importance of research designs that address the issues of concern to local decision makers and practitioners. They argue that effective evaluations produce both practice-based knowledge of how the technology integration process can best meet locally defined learning goals in schools and research-based knowledge concerning which technological applications can work best in which educational environments.

The authors assert that when student learning does improve in schools that become technology-rich, those gains are not caused solely by the presence of technology or by isolated technology-learner interactions. Rather, such changes are the result of an ecological shift and are grounded in a set of changes in the learning environment that prioritize and focus a district's or school's core educational objectives. For some districts, this may mean a focus on literacy; for others, it may be using technology to support high-level scientific inquiry. The authors have seen that technology does not just bring change to a static set of tasks (such as typing on a keyboard instead of writing on paper, or searching the Internet rather than an encyclopedia). Rather, technology enhances the communicative, expressive, analytic, and logistical capabilities of the teaching and learning environment.

Technologies can support ways of learning that would otherwise be difficult to achieve. They involve qualities like dynamic and relevant communication with people outside of the classroom and habitual revision and reworking of original student work, written or otherwise. Technologies can support activities that many believe are learning experiences that all students should have in all schools, activities such as visualizing complex scientific data, accessing primary historical source materials, and representing one's work to multiple audiences. It is this broadly defined quality of technology-rich learning and teaching experiences that the authors place at the core of their research agenda.

Culp et al. treat technology as a crucial player in a complex process of change that cannot be accomplished by technological fixes alone. They believe that stakeholders are not just interested in narrow proofs of technology's impacts on student achievement but rather are open to alternative, more realistic explanations of the role technology can play in schools. The authors believe that these stakeholders can best be spoken to by research that addresses the following issues:

- How technology is integrated into educational settings
- How new electronic resources are interpreted and adapted by their users
- How technological capacities can best be matched with students' learning needs
- How technological change can interact with and support changes in other aspects of the educational process, such as assessment, administration, communication, and curriculum development

The guiding question for these authors is "How can researchers act as mediators, synthesizing the findings of locally generated evaluations to inform policy?" The authors respond to this question by linking together two goals: finding scalable and substantive ways to support local school communities in thinking differently about evaluative questions and about evidence; and finding equally substantive and effective ways to synthesize and disseminate local findings to a much broader policy community.

Culp et al. conclude that evaluation research that is responsive to local concerns, constraints, and priorities can be structured and synthesized to produce knowledge about effective uses of educational technology. This effort would be facilitated by a network of intermediary research organizations working to review, synthesize, and generalize from locally generated evaluation studies, producing broad-based findings that could guide large-scale policy making. By building up from many small-scale studies that focus on particular technologies used in the service of particular learning goals, and by taking local contextual factors into account, researchers could have greater confidence that their findings are capturing relevant local variations as well as addressing questions about the particular features and claims associated with particular technologies.

Under this scheme, the authors argue, the locally focused studies would have a high level of face validity within their local communities and still be able to inform the much larger scale projects of policymakers. The authors refer to this approach as *partnership research* and propose the use of a network of Technology Evaluation Teams that would research a prioritized set of thematic areas. Each team would be made up of researchers focused on a set of thematic or disciplinary areas identified as high priorities within the larger project of determining the effectiveness of technology in education.

RETHINKING EVALUATION FOR TECHNOLOGY INNOVATIONS

In their chapter, "A Distributed Evaluation Model," Eva L. Baker and Joan L. Herman of UCLA's Center for Research and Evaluation on Standards and Student Testing (CRESST) arrive at a somewhat similar recommendation through a different chain of reasoning. They begin with the assertion that current evaluation approaches and student learning measures are ill suited for evaluating contemporary learning technology implementations. They document the purposes and challenges involved in the evaluation of technological advances intended for use in education. They describe the range of purposes thought to be served by formal evaluations (e.g., justifying expenditures, providing comparisons both with conventional practice and with plausible alternatives, studying how an innovation is implemented) and characterize common associated evaluation approaches. Some evaluations intend to answer what are called *summative* questions about whether something had positive effects; others focus on *formative* issues of how to improve the treatment and its implementation.

Although random assignment to contrasting technology treatments is theoretically possible, Baker and Herman argue that in practice it is very difficult to pull off. Impediments include parental demands for equal access to technology, individual teachers' varying interest in and comfort with implementing technology, and differential home support and resources for technology use. As a result, many evaluations settle for student and teacher opinions about the technology—measures that the authors characterize as the "smile test."

Other obstacles to effective evaluations of technology include its rapid pace of change, the fact that intended outcomes are often unclear or vary across settings, and the difficulty in obtaining appropriate student learning measures. Baker and Herman argue that evaluators are caught between two suboptimal choices. They can examine performance on standardized tests, but the tests' content often is not relevant to the technology innovation being evaluated. On the other hand, they can use assessments created by the technology developers for their system; but these assessments, while relevant, often lack the technical qualities needed for rigorous quantitative analysis.

The authors believe that, in contrast to current practice, credible evaluations in this field will require a set of conditions specific to the evaluation of technology. These conditions include the availability of the technology; the support of management; skilled implementation of the technology innovation by teachers; students with the necessary prior knowledge and skills; and appropriate timing and integration of the technology innovation in the curriculum.

After laying bare the limits of familiar evaluation approaches, Baker and Herman put forth a model of technology evaluation that they argue is an evolution of current practice. Their approach, which they call *distributed evaluation,* attempts to serve both formative and summative purposes, and has several distinctive features:

- A clear, shared understanding of the evaluation's purposes and goals on the part of all participants
- The use of common measures (*indicators*) across different implementations as well as flexible measures that can reflect local implementations
- Longitudinal designs in which students, teachers, classes, or schools are followed over time
- Distributed data collection and analysis
- Reporting to all audiences in easy-to-understand graphic or iconic displays

Baker and Herman provide an example of distributed evaluation in their ongoing evaluation of a diverse set of distance learning courses that were developed at various institutions in a variety of contexts.

PUTTING THE APPROACHES INTO PERSPECTIVE

The researchers represented in this section present vastly different views concerning the research approaches most appropriate in evaluating the effects of technology on student learning. These differences reflect their different experiences and forms of expertise, and also differences in their view of the important question or questions an evaluation must answer. Promoters of randomized experiments emphasize the detection of causal relationships between interventions and effects. The other researcher groups have been more concerned with answering "local" questions of practitioners, on the one hand, and with building a complex model of the local education system and the way that the introduction of a technology-supported innovation influences (and is influenced by) that system, on the other. We close this section with comments on the chapters from reviewers representing two important outside perspectives. Nick Smith, professor of education at Syracuse University, and the current President of the American Evaluation Association, brings to this task the perspective of an experienced evaluator who has used a range of methodologies and designs. Julia A. Stapleton, formerly the director of educational technology for the state of New Jersey, reviews these research discussions for their usefulness to state and district policymakers who are called on both to sponsor and to consume such evaluations. Both of these commentators identify issues that policymakers, including district and school administrators, confront as they participate in the funding, interpretation, and dissemination of evaluations.

Evaluating Educational Technology Research Designs from a Policy Perspective

Julia A. Stapleton

Schools are moving forward vigorously to infuse educational technology into the instructional process. The evidence of increased technology access is overwhelming. New Jersey's statistics are an example of this increase. In 1994, the ratio of students to all instructional computers in New Jersey was 15:1. In 2001, 4.5:1 is the average student to multi-media computer ratio in New Jersey's public schools (Public School Technology Survey, 2001). New Jersey is not alone. According to the May 2001 issue of Education Week's Technology Counts, the ratio of students nationwide to instructional, multimedia computers is 7.9:1 and the ratio of students to all instructional computers is 4.9:1. In 1994 that ratio for students to all instructional computers was 10.8:1.

Thus student access to technology resources is increasing. As the educational technology director for the New Jersey Department of Education from 1995–2002, I continually sought ways to demonstrate how, why, and where technology is having an impact on student learning. For any agency responsible for promoting the implementation of educational technology, it seems prudent and necessary to gauge the effectiveness of what has been implemented in enabling students to achieve educational goals.

Given the many variables in educational settings and the inherent complexity of technology, the questions that need to be addressed in evaluations of educational technology are many. They include the following:

- Does access to technology have an effect on teaching and learning?
- Is the effect measurable on standardized achievement tests?
- What are the benefits and challenges when technology is infused into curricula?
- How do technology access and use impact the roles, functions, and expertise of teachers and students?
- What is the impact of technology-supported activities on student learning?
- How are student-centered technology-supported activities managed in the classroom?
- How important is professional development for teachers?
- Does technology access and use result in change to the system or organization?
- How much time is sufficient to determine measurable changes from technology implementation?
- What are the most effective technologies in the instructional process?
- How does the infusion of technology significantly impact the goals of learning—or, do the learning goals significantly impact technology infusion?

These questions cover a broad range of topics and issues highlighting just how difficult it is to evaluate technology. Before commenting on the various potential methods for evaluating educational technology, I will describe some events in the state of New Jersey that influenced my beliefs about how evaluations can assist policymakers and educators.

EDUCATIONAL TECHNOLOGY IN NEW JERSEY

In 1996–97 New Jersey laws were passed and partnerships formed to implement educational technology programs for the state's more than 2,300 K–12 public schools, serving 1.3 million students.

The *Comprehensive Educational Improvement and Financing Act of 1996* led the way by allocating nearly $275 million in state funds for 5 years (1997–2002) to be distributed as Distance Learning Network Aid on a per-pupil basis. Recognizing the importance of professional development to support this investment, New Jersey law [P.L.1996, c.129] called for the establishment of Educational Technology Training Centers (ETTCs). Twenty-one ETTCs (one per county) began operation on July 1, 1997.

In 1997 the Board of Public Utilities, the New Jersey Ratepayer Advocate, the New Jersey Department of Education, and Bell Atlantic forged an agreement that led to the adoption of Access New Jersey (ANJ). The ANJ program included a commitment of $80 million over 4 years (1997–2001) to provide discounts ranging from 33–72 percent for high-speed telecommunications services and free customer-premise equipment.

School districts were required to develop technology plans that were guided by the New Jersey Department of Education's newly adopted vision and educational technology goals. The department's vision was that all students, no matter which district's schools they attended, would be able to achieve the New Jersey Core Curriculum Content Standards because they would have unlimited access to people, to the vast array of curriculum and instruction offered in the state, and to information and ideas, no matter where they existed.

On the national level increased support came at the same time when the Federal Communications Commission (FCC) adopted rules in 1997 to implement the Universal Service Fund, or E-rate, which enabled schools and libraries to receive significant discounts on all telecommunications services. The fund is around $2.25 billion per year. (New Jersey schools averaged about $42 million per year from the E-rate.) At the same time, the U.S. Department of Education's Technology Literacy Challenge Fund (TLCF) offered funding to all states for competitive grants to Local Education Agencies (LEA) over a 5-year period (1997–2001). (New Jersey averaged about $9 million per year from TLCF.) Hence state goals, federal and state programs, local district technology plans, and fiscal resources enabling technology access came together and encouraged schools in New Jersey to embrace the implementation of technology.

To measure the state's progress on the state's technology goals, the department initiated the school technology survey in 1999. Three years of survey data indicated that the department had fully or substantially attained the state's educational technology goals by the end of the 2000–01 school year (Public School Technology Survey, 2001). For example, for the goal that all teachers have the skills and knowledge needed to use technology as an effective tool to support achievement of the state's Core Curriculum Content Standards, progress was evident, as shown in Table 1.1.

Teacher responses to survey items concerning their technology capabilities were used to classify teachers according to their level of technology proficiency, using the standards established by the International Society for Technology in Education (ISTE). Given the fact that we expected systemic change to take from 3–5 years, these annual increases in teacher proficiency were heartening.

Table 1.1. New Jersey Teachers' Proficiency Levels

Year of Survey	Teacher Proficiency Levels			
	Beginner	Intermediate	Advanced	Instructor
1999	35.5%	41.1%	18.4%	5.9%
2000	30.4%	46.2%	20.4%	6.4%
2001	26.1%	48.6%	21.5%	6.8%

Evaluating Union City's Technology Efforts

While there are many school districts in New Jersey where technology is an important component in driving systemic change, I have chosen to relate the experiences of the Union City School District to illustrate the impact of a successful technology program and the importance of its evaluation.

Like many urban school districts, Union City faced serious educational challenges. Union City was identified by the state as a special needs district, because of poverty levels and other unique characteristics. The city has more than 60,000 residents packed into one square mile of land. More than 90% of Union City's residents speak English as a second language. This district has been classified as one of the nation's 92 most impoverished communities.

In the early 1990s, the Union City School District received failing marks in 44 of the 52 categories that the New Jersey Department of Education used to assess schools. They were at serious risk of a takeover by the department. The threat prompted many changes in Union City, including a technological transformation.

In 1992 Bell Atlantic (now Verizon) responded to Union City's partnership appeal and offered to work with them to demonstrate how technology could be used to improve student performance. A technology trial, entitled Project Explore, began in September 1993. Computers were installed in the Christopher Columbus Middle School and at the homes of all 135 seventh-grade students and their teachers at the onset of Project Explore. The access to technology enabled students and their parents to communicate between school and home, and to have basic software tools to carry out curriculum activities.

Project Explore equipped every classroom in the school with computers. Professional development and parental involvement were key components of the program. Curriculum guides were rewritten to support the development of thinking, reasoning, and collaboration skills in all content areas. Students learned by doing, using technology and demonstrating their proficiencies via research papers and hands-on projects. Carefully documented by the Center for Children and Technology (CCT), the results of Project Explore were impressive (Honey & Henriquez, 1996). The results of this trial included a marked improvement in standardized test scores and in writing skills, significant declines in absenteeism, and a jump in the number of students transferring into the school.

Union City Online was the next step. A major purpose of this program is to develop and measure the success of a technical infrastructure that delivers high-speed Internet connectivity to all 11 schools in the district. Union City Online served as a test bed to learn about the dynamics of technology integration and educational reform. The project was supported by the National Science Foundation, Bell Atlantic/Verizon, and the Center for Children and Technology. The CCT report of April 1998 details the range of factors, both contextual and technology-facilitated, that has made a difference in students' performances throughout the district (Chang et al., 1998). Key aspects of Union City's success included teachers at the center of curricular revision and support from the district leadership. Today Union City's students score more than 10 points above the statewide average on standardized tests, while in 1990 their scores were significantly below state averages.

Thus, from the early stages of technology implementation, the district's leaders recognized the importance of evaluation—measuring achievements and challenges in partnership with CCT. Union City's success with educational technology and systemic improvement has been documented and reported worldwide in the media, through presentations via major documents and on-line resources.

The influx of educational technology in New Jersey roughly paralleled similar developments in many states throughout the nation in the late 1990s. At the school district level, however, Union City School District's programs and evaluation process preceded developments elsewhere. Hence the questions raised and methods framed in Union City serve as an evaluation foundation for the educational community.

Despite the progress made in Union City, there is still a need for advances in how evaluation of technology is done in schools. As the infrastructure grows and technology resources are woven into instructional activities on a daily basis, the effects of technology on student achievement must be understood.

ALTERNATIVE EVALUATION APPROACHES

Given the rapidly evolving uses of technology in classrooms, it is a daunting task to identify appropriate evaluation designs or models that measure the impact of educational technology on teachers' instructional practices and students' achievement.

As a policymaker, I need to sponsor research designs that are compatible with the conditions inherent in the use of technology for instructional purposes. Moreover, I want research designs to provide answers to the many questions associated with using technology effectively; these go beyond the question of "what works," as indicated in the list of questions at the opening of this commentary.

Of the chapters in *Evaluating Educational Technology* that I reviewed, two recommend that the data collection be designed to include such items as information about teachers' and students' prior experiences and attitudes about technology. Collecting data about technology infrastructure, along with curriculum and technical support within a school, are also deemed important in these chapters. As a state policymaker, I agree wholeheartedly. The lack of curriculum support and technical expertise within the school setting can reduce the richest technology environments to ineffectiveness.

Contextualized Evaluation Approaches

The more "contextualized" research approaches are attractive in that they respond to, rather than control, the role of technology in the complex activity of schooling. As in the Union City case discussed earlier, close working relationships between research teams and districts and schools can help policymakers discern whether or not their changes are on track. Authors promoting designs capturing context variables demonstrate their awareness of the multiple factors impinging on technology use in practice, such as equipment availability, management support, skilled implementation by teachers, students' prior knowledge and skills, and appropriate timing and integration in the curriculum—all major concerns of stakeholders.

Two of the chapters in the research volume provide for capturing these contextual variables in a way that is sensitive to stakeholders in individual locations while still accumulating findings across multiple evaluations—namely those by Baker and Herman and by Culp, Honey, and Spielvogel.

In both chapters, I found information that resolved many concerns that I have raised over the years about appropriate and effective educational technology evaluation methods. For example, it is important that the research design enable the rapid release of the results back to the practitioners to support their understanding of the effects of the intervention and the resulting change process. Their designs address these needs for timely communication among evaluators and practitioners. Moreover, both chapters outline how the continual evolution of technology innovations can play havoc with any serious study. Evaluation of this evolving field must be a process-based approach, not an analytically controlled study of a single factor over a short term.

The features of Baker and Herman's distributed evaluation include indicators with common classes of questions and flexible measures, network-based data collection and distribution, and feedback to all audiences. Their stated desire is to design an evaluation that is directly relevant, targeted and useful to improvement. But they also recognize that there are no easy answers to the accurate measurement of educational technology's impact on students' learning.

Culp, Honey, and Spielvogel propose institutionalizing a process that weaves together local questions and large-scale policy needs through the creation of a network of Technology Evaluation Teams. This model is intended to generate robust findings about effectiveness of the technology use in the high-priority areas, speed the availability of research and evaluation back to the practitioner to make informed decisions, and guide the change process through the synthesis of many local research studies or findings. This synthesis of best practices could be very valuable to policymakers and practitioners—as long as the link between the practices and student achievement is clear.

To be effective, the Technology Evaluation Teams would have to be systemically adopted by policymakers at regional centers throughout the nation. I doubt that widespread adoption will be forthcoming unless practitioners and stakeholders become convinced that the activities of the Technology Evaluation Teams would provide answers to questions about the effectiveness of technology in improving student performance on standardized tests.

Experimental Designs

The alternative to designs stressing contextual variables and sensitivity to local stakeholder concerns involves tightly controlled experiments. It is clear that randomized field trials or experiments have been effective in many domains in providing answers to questions about effectiveness. Cook, Means, Haertel, and Michalchik's discussion of setting up experimental and control conditions for technology studies was revealing because the focus appears to be on the treatment while ignoring the variables inherent in dealing with individual people. The complexity of issues when students, teachers, and technology are involved is such that I suspect this kind of experimenter control is impossible in most educational technology settings.

Randomized experiments have yet to be accepted by the educational community as relevant to measuring the effects of technology. Why? As many of the research papers point out, while randomized samples are theoretically possible, they are very difficult to accomplish with the many variables associated with educational technology. Variables include technology's differential allure to individual teachers, coupled with the multiple factors associated with varied classroom implementations. The diversity of school settings, coupled with the complexity of technology, confound attempts at clean designs that can yield clear findings.

Thus I began reading the research design chapters with skepticism concerning the relevance of random-assignment experiments to this field. After reading the chapters, however, I became convinced that experiments could be productively used by the educational community to learn about the effects of *specific* uses of educational technology. The hypothetical experimental design proposed by Cook et al. deals with samples of 11th graders, who would conduct 10 research projects in American history over a period of one semester. In considering the hypothetical experiment, the authors address the complexity of variables related to technology's impact. For example, they note that effects depend on variables such as abundance and quality of the on-line content, student engagement, and teacher coaching. While I do not think it is feasible for researchers to control educational technology use *in general* or over the long term, as they would need to in order to conduct a controlled experiment, I did become persuaded that well-defined short-term technology practices could be studied through experiments.

General Concerns

A major concern for all the designs described here is their ability to address the evolving nature and rapid cycle times of technology. There is a serious risk that by the time of study completion the technology applications in the study will be no longer relevant. Several of the paper authors (notably Baker and Herman and Culp et al.) sought to address this concern, but their strategies for increasing the timeliness of research remain unproven.

CONCLUSION

These chapters provide blueprints for credible design elements in measuring the effects of educational technology. Yet the authors recognize that the very nature of technology in education can create havoc with any research design. Research designs for technology's effectiveness must take into consideration multiple factors such as the diversity of schools, the uniqueness of educators' approaches, the variety of student learning styles, time, and rapidly changing technology tools. To counter the challenge posed by technology's natural complexity within school settings, the authors—in varying degrees—address diversity and defend their designs as overcoming these intrinsic characteristics of educational technology.

The evaluation of educational technology is important to policymakers, practitioners, and stakeholders. The multiple variants associated with using educational technology in schools should not discourage evaluators and researchers. The challenges associated with creating valid evaluation designs are not insurmountable. Evidence of this is provided in Chapters 1–4 in *Evaluating Educational Technology*. These chapters examine important research and design issues, and the proposals they make may help to elucidate how to determine the effectiveness of educational technology programs.

One criticism of the chapters is their failure to specify timelines for their models. As a policymaker, I am constantly asked to link the effectiveness of the instructional design to student performance. This takes time. When technology is involved, how much time is dependent on many variables, such as the complexity of the implementation strategy, the proficiency of the instructors and learners, and the availability of appropriate infrastructure and tools to effectively make a change. Indeed, there must be sufficient time to measure student achievement on a continuum that involves at least three yearlong cycles, especially if an annual achievement test is to be the measure. I am hopeful that each design will incorporate sufficient time to address systemic change and formally measure this change with relevant student performance indicators.

Given their application over a sufficient time frame (or after implementations have had an opportunity to mature), research designs such as those described in *Evaluating Educational Technology* could enable and extend the ability of policymakers and practitioners to determine the effectiveness of educational technology practices. This information is very useful in convincing legislators and stakeholders to invest in educational technology and its evaluation. For example, Cook at al.'s randomized experimental research design with American history classrooms could (depending on the outcome) convince investors that every classroom should have Internet access. Similarly, the results of large-scale, consolidated efforts with data collected on specific areas (such as early grades literacy or English as a second language technology interventions) of the sort described in Culp et al.'s chapter could convince schools to consolidate resources and coordinate efforts to provide teams of evaluators to address their own research initiatives in targeted areas. Hence local and state efforts could be addressing a set of thematic or disciplinary areas identified as high priorities in their area. By combining and sharing this data, all policymakers would benefit from the investment and, more important, would have relevant data to determine what are essential technologies for student learning.

All of the questions posed at the beginning of this piece cannot be answered with one research design or method. When stakeholders want information on multiple factors collected over an extended period of time, it would appear that the models emphasizing contextual variables would serve well. Randomized experiments would appear to be more appropriate when there is less concern with understanding the influence of contextual variables and the time frame for the intervention is limited. Applying any of these research designs should increase the capacity of local school districts and state departments of education to accurately measure the effectiveness of educational technology practices. The results should also enable stakeholders to make decisions about what practices should be continued and what might be eliminated. Hence the evaluation process could result in more effective and efficient data-driven decisions that serve to better inform policymakers as they decide on future technology investments. Evaluation is an investment in the future success of any program.

Research Designs to Evaluate Technology Innovations: Alternative Approaches

Nick L. Smith

Two themes will surface repeatedly in this commentary: how the various authors of three of the chapters in *Evaluating Educational Technology: Effective Research Designs for Improving Learning* (namely, Cook, Means, Haertel, & Michalchik, Chap. 1; Culp, Honey, & Spielvogel, Chap. 3; and Baker & Herman, Chap. 4) envision the proper role of research and evaluation in studying educational technology, and how they treat the issue of technology itself. These themes illuminate the general positions of the authors, highlight the strengths and weaknesses of their arguments, and provide a basis for comparing the different positions taken.

In assessing the different inquiry designs advocated across these chapters, it is important to recognize the implicit definitions of evaluation employed by the various authors. In several places, the authors seem to equate evaluation with research, specifically causal research; this is the general position of Cook et al. Under this view, evaluation is defined in terms of the kinds of questions asked, with causal questions taken to be of most importance. Questions of value ("Is A good? Is A better than B?") are reinterpreted as questions of causation ("Does A work? Does A work better than B?"). It is understandable that these would be the primary questions of the educational technologist and the educational researcher, but, as recognized at points in these chapters, it is less clear that these are, or even should be, the primary questions of the parent, the teacher, the school administrator, or the policymaker, when they ask for rigorous evidence of the impact of technology.

If evaluation of technology is seen as less a matter of research and more a matter of addressing the information needs of various client groups, then instead of focusing on which causal questions to ask, one might seek to identify what questions clients are concerned about and what types of answers they consider relevant. In this view, the client's questions are the most important ones to address, not the researchers'. This is more the point of view of Culp et al. and especially of Baker and Herman.

Not all effects of technology are necessarily instructional effects. Clients may be concerned with instructional, causal issues, but may sometimes be more concerned with noncausal issues such as matters of social justice or program sustainability. Parents and policymakers may view technology as a societal and educational resource and be concerned about the social equity of its access and use in terms of social class, cultural, sexual, and racial bias. School administrators may be concerned about the financial, political, and organizational sustainability of technological innovations when scarce resources must be allocated across competing demands. While researchers might interpret the value question of "Is A good?" in terms of "Does A work?" parents might interpret that question in terms of "Is A compatible with our family values?" and "Does A improve our community?" School administrators might interpret the question as "Is A financially viable?" and "Does A foster political support for our school?" Rigorous designs are needed to address these questions as well.

It is important to recognize that convincing arguments in favor of using experiments to evaluate educational technology rest on the premise that causal questions are of paramount interest. This may not always be the case, for example, when teachers and parents see the latest technology as an implicit educational entitlement (Haertel & Means, 2003), when school administrators are more concerned with short-term, comparative advantage of alternative changing technologies than with absolute measures of technology impact, and when policymakers are concerned with universal, politically acceptable, marginal improvements to public education. In educational technology, the "evaluation of effects" can be construed more broadly than simply causal research on instructional impact. Proponents of experimental designs seem to suggest that policy decisions are based primarily on the quality of empirical evidence rather than on political self-interest, economic profit, or competing social values. This latter consideration is especially important in education where what constitutes "good education" is often in much greater dispute than what constitutes "good health" in medical research.

EVALUATING THE CASE FOR RANDOMIZED EXPERIMENTS

In their chapter "The Case for Randomized Experiments," Cook et al. acknowledge that there are noncausal questions of importance in studying educational technology, but focus on causal questions as most often of primary concern, and on randomized experiments because they provide answers that are "better epistemologically warranted, more efficient, and more respected in policy and social science circles" than alternatives (p. 16). Although they agree that the study of causal mediating processes allows one to transfer knowledge to new applications and should be incorporated into experiments when possible, they emphasize causal description, not causal explanation: the study of what works, but not necessarily how it works (which is often a major concern of instructional designers and teachers developing remedial materials when new technologies fail to have the promised effects).

Cook et al. present a procedurally detailed, but hypothetical, example to support their position that the proper focus of a technology experiment is not a study of a particular piece of software, nor a study of a complex set of technological influences, but an alternative-interventions study in which a specific treatment can be grounded in substantive theory, outcomes can be clearly identified and carefully measured, and subjects can be appropriately assigned to treatment conditions.

The chapter then abruptly moves to respond to major objections to the use of experiments in evaluation (including oversimplified theory of causation, oversimplified epistemology, unsuitability to complex organizations, inadequate program theory, political infeasibility, failed prior attempts, unacceptable trade-offs, and unethical random assignment), arguing that the objections are exaggerated and do not undermine the fundamental utility of the experiment in answering descriptive causal questions of impact. This analysis evenhandedly clarifies issues and distinctions; it clearly acknowledges the limitations of the experimental approach while persuasively arguing for its wider application. The problems of employing experimental designs are discussed in such detail and at such length, however, that even the reader who wants to believe in their more general use is likely to become discouraged. The benefits are abstract and theoretical; the problems are real, concrete, and apparently formidable for even the most experienced evaluators—this is not likely to encourage local school evaluators to attempt controlled experiments.

Cook et al. seem to argue that randomized selection of study participants is so rarely possible as to be hardly worth consideration. This is a serious blow to the argument in favor of experimentation, given how important randomized selection is to claims that a study's results will generalize to the population as a whole and hence should guide policy formation. They advocate, instead, multiple randomized assignment studies, a recommendation that will further discourage school districts from doing experiments because of the substantial time, control, and resources required.

The argument in support of descriptive causal studies could have been more compelling. Too little attention is paid to examples illustrating how the experimental approach has worked in evaluating educational technology. A few success stories would have provided a more balanced and encouraging presentation. Attention is not even drawn back to how the objections to randomized experiments reviewed here might be overcome in the hypothetical example presented earlier in the chapter. Without such positive examples, the skeptical reader might conclude that randomized studies are too infeasible to ever be widely used. Cook et al. argue that school administrators could be induced to comply with the considerable organizational restrictions required to conduct randomized experiments through the use of incentives, but the specific incentives are not described. Nor is there any evidence that these incentives would be sufficient to induce a school or district to stick with their assigned condition over time in the face of turnover in principals, superintendents, and school board members.

Cook et al. next consider four alternative designs that have been proposed as superior to the randomized experiment: designs emphasizing qualitative hypothesis discovery over quantitative hypothesis testing, designs for studying the mediating processes specified in a substantive program theory (i.e., causal modeling), quasi-experimental designs, and design experiments. They conclude that these designs "deserve to be treated as adjuncts to experiments rather than as alternatives to them" (Cook et al., 2003, p. 35).

It would have been instructive to identify how using each of these design alternatives would have produced a less satisfactory result in the hypothetical technology evaluation study presented earlier in the chapter.

THOUGHTS ON ACHIEVING RELEVANCE AND INFLUENCE

Cook et al. emphasize single and multiple randomized studies of technology designed to answer basic, policy-relevant questions of impact. They say less about how the characteristics of technology and its use in education shape their design decisions. In the chapter "Achieving Local Relevance and Broader Influence," Culp et al. discuss the educational, social, and organizational contexts within which technology is used in the schools, and propose that, with proper support, the knowledge produced by locally relevant evaluations can be used to guide large-scale policy making. They report that, although their earlier work employed design experiments within a cognitive science, causal modeling orientation, experience has led them to an approach that is more collaborative, sensitive to local differences, and attentive to the important social and political influences that shape technology use and impact. They propose a method for conducting local evaluations called Partnership Research, which emphasizes collaboration with teachers and administrators, is sensitive to locally felt needs and challenges, attends to goals both locally important and informative to a larger community, and learns from the complexities of real school situations. Unfortunately, procedural details of how to design such studies are not provided.

Culp et al. propose "a national organizational infrastructure that could serve as a mediating presence for practitioners, researchers, and policymakers, both synthesizing locally grounded research to inform policy, and supporting critical consumption of research information among practitioners" (p. 82). They propose a network of state or regional Technology Evaluation Teams of researchers focused on different thematic areas within educational technology (such as how technology can improve instruction in high school science or in English as a second language). Researchers in the teams would synthesize and disseminate research in their domain; develop key research questions; create research methods and instruments and share them with local researchers; support local researchers; collect and review local research, synthesizing it in collaboration with other researchers.

Although the avowed purpose of this organizational structure is to support local participants, it seems to focus more on the interests of the team researchers themselves. Few details are provided about how this process is to be managed, how information is to be synthesized, and especially how local researchers are to be supported to be able to produce knowledge of adequate quality to be worth synthesizing for broader use and policy making. This is a key issue, since the synthesis of locally produced knowledge is the essence of the proposal, and the only local researchers described in the chapter are high school teachers. If the authors of the other chapters are correct about how difficult it is to produce valid, useful, and generalizeable knowledge about the use and impact of educational technology, then most high school teachers are not likely to have the needed training and experience; a remarkable system of local support would seem to be needed.

COMMENTS ON A DISTRIBUTED EVALUATION MODEL

In contrast to the previous two chapters, Baker and Herman (2003) begin their chapter, "A Distributed Evaluation Model," with a discussion of the nature of educational technology and its evaluation, focusing on what is known from prior efforts about the adequacy of study designs to answer a range of implementation, formative revision, and impact (both quality, i.e., evaluation, and mechanism, i.e., research) questions. They review the problems in technology evaluation of unsatisfactory conceptions of evaluation, practical constraints on design implementation, and inadequate measurement. They portray educational technology as a rapidly evolving, multilayered, contextually determined, educational-social-organizational phenomenon, for which any existing evaluation approach is unsuited. They note, "Of particular concern in the evaluation of technology is whether or not there is anything like a stable treatment to be assessed, and if so, for how long" (p. 106).

Their solution is to move from designs for a specific evaluation study, or series of studies, to a design for an evaluation system. The four attributes of their proposed model, called Distributed Evaluation, include (1) evaluation purposes and goals understood by all (evaluators, sponsors, administrators, teachers, students), (2) a longitudinal design employing both common and site-specific measurement indicators, (3) responsibility for data collection and analysis distributed to local sites, and (4) feedback distributed to all participants (evaluators, sponsors, administrators, teachers, students).

Although Baker and Herman sketch how such a system might work, they do not provide much justification that such a massive, complex, long-term system is feasible within most public school systems. What is proposed is a major organizational intervention to construct an elaborate management information system, an innovation likely to take months, if not years, to successfully implement. Given the considerable practical problems recounted by Cook et al. in implementing short-term, highly focused randomized experiments in schools, one would expect even greater difficulty in implementing this more elaborate system.

Baker and Herman effectively reflect the dynamic, locally defined nature of educational technology, but the evaluation system they propose seems too elaborate and cumbersome to provide responsive, cost-effective, high-quality information; one would expect an evaluation strategy that was more light, fluid, and transparent. They suggest that their system is possible based on technological improvements—as yet not fully realized—in indicator development and Web-based communications. They also report that an instance of their Distributed Evaluation system exists and is under trial, but more detail is needed to fully understand the system.

Many school districts already collect more data than they have the time, resources, or expertise to effectively use. Perhaps a less resource-demanding version of the model proposed here by Baker and Herman, incorporated in a district's current information system, might be an effective way to increase that district's yield of available evaluation information.

FINAL REFLECTIONS

The chapters describing alternative learning technology evaluation approaches offer important suggestions for how to improve the quality of information about the impact of educational technology. The views range from controlled experimental studies to locally supportive information systems, to a national structure for synthesizing and disseminating research knowledge. A wide range of evaluator roles are suggested: evaluator as researcher, as facilitator, and as partner. Although numerous procedural details and practical problems remain to be addressed, each chapter offers an important alternative for consideration.

In terms of technology, Cook et al. do not seem to take a particular position either for or against educational technology, but simply view it as an important phenomenon to be studied. Baker and Herman, and Culp et al. are much less neutral. These latter authors describe technology as, at a minimum, an inescapable aspect of present and future educational life, and, ideally, as a powerful tool to be exploited in the improvement of education. Fundamentally, they are technology advocates, not unbiased evaluators of the utility, dangers, benefits, and costs of technology. They advocate implementation research designed to promote the widespread use of technology. They are probably less likely to raise questions of "whether?" being more interested in questions of "how?" Have they traded the researcher's and evaluator's detachment for the true belief of the developer, becoming more concerned with what is possible than what is useful?

As technology researchers, Cook et al. tend to construe technology in terms of instructional alternatives and present explicit study designs for answering descriptive causal questions of instructional impact. These are well-tested approaches, but much easier to describe than to successfully implement. As technology advocates, Baker and Herman and Culp et al. view technology as more than instructional alternatives, and evaluation as more than descriptive causal research. They portray technology as a complex, rapidly changing social and educational enterprise. They propose design strategies for complicated, interconnected systems, at this time envisioned but not fully realized. The development of designs for evaluating technology is clearly a "work in progress," and work needs to progress on each of the alternatives proposed in these chapters.

All of the chapters in this section seek to provide inquiry designs that are both rigorous and useful; it is the trade-off among different values that produces such a provocative range of alternative designs for studying technology impacts. As a collection, however, these chapters give priority to designs that are primarily rigorous and useful in answering the questions of researchers.

Policymakers might benefit more from new policy analysis and needs assessment designs that help track the widespread effects of technology innovation, use, and impact in terms of cost, social justice, cultural relevance, and political and economic sustainability. Practitioners might be better served by strategies which are much more adaptive and cost-effective than those proposed here. They need designs that are flexible and responsive to changing technology variations and local information needs, and to shifting time, resource, and talent constraints. They need design strategies of modest cost that provide relatively quick turnaround, with information of sufficient quality to make marginal improvements in emerging technology decisions.

Although no designs reported in these chapters satisfy these constraints, such radical departures from current practice are possible. For example, evaluation methodologists have solved similarly challenging design problems, such as with the innovative development of the Service Delivery Assessment approaches now used effectively in many of the federal offices of Inspectors General (Hendricks, 1982; Hendricks, Mangano, and Moran, 1990). Similar design creativity is now needed in the evaluation of educational technology.

PART II

NEED FOR RELEVANT MEASURES OF STUDENT LEARNING

With the passage of the NCLB legislation in 2001, policymakers and administrators making decisions about implementing technology in elementary and secondary schools became subject to a stronger degree of accountability than ever before. The legislation provides for an Educational Technology State Grants Program, which channels federal monies to states for distribution to high-need districts for the purpose of implementing educational technology. The states and districts are required to use these funds only for "research-based" technology integration strategies and curricula. Further, participating states and districts are held accountable for demonstrating that the technology strategies are helping students meet "challenging state academic standards." Thus local education agencies using federal funds to support technology integration must provide assessment data demonstrating progress on selected state academic standards.

A key factor affecting the ability of states and districts to demonstrate progress on challenging academic standards will be the way in which student performance is assessed. In this section of the book, we consider issues surrounding the match between the intended learning outcomes, the technology-supported intervention intended to enhance students' attainment of those outcomes, and the nature of the tests or other assessments used to measure student learning.

TECHNOLOGY CAN BE USED FOR MANY PURPOSES

Some technology proponents argue that asking for research demonstrating the educational benefits of information technology is akin to asking for research showing the educational benefits of the pencil. Both are tools that can be used for a wide range of purposes and under many different circumstances. We cannot evaluate the impact of technology per se; instead, we must define more specific practices incorporating particular technology tools or supports and evaluate the effects of these. Some classrooms use computers to support young writers, with the belief that they will be more motivated to write extended text and, especially, to edit their writing, when supported by word processing software and the ability to print clean, professional-looking copies of their work. Some teachers use action-filled, computer-based math games as a way to fill time for students who have finished their textbook-based mathematics assignments; other teachers use the same games as a way to provide extra practice for students who are struggling with computation. Some high school science classrooms provide students with the opportunity to explore images of outer space, learning how to classify different types of galaxies, and even to discover heretofore-unknown stars. Clearly, it would make little sense to assess student learning in all these classrooms with the same test. Equally clearly, we are unlikely to find any effects of using technology to support learning if the assessment has nothing to do with the learning experience at hand.

As obvious as this maxim seems, it is one that appears to be violated commonly in practice. In most states the academic subject areas on which students are tested repeatedly are reading and mathematics, and this trend will only intensify now with passage of the NCLB legislation. To receive federal educational funds, a state must test every public school student in reading and mathematics every year from the third through the eighth grades on a nationally normed test. Given the prominence of these assessments in federal, state, and local accountability systems, some policymakers are frank in stating that they have little interest in any educational innovation that will not raise reading and mathematics scores.

Clearly, the purchase of computers and wiring of schools for Internet access in and of themselves will not raise students' reading and mathematics test scores. The impact on those tests will depend upon how the technology infrastructure is used with students. Some educational technology is designed to teach the kinds of reading skills and mathematics procedures that are covered on standardized tests. If a technology infrastructure is used to provide students with extended use of such software, positive effects on scores on tests of reading and computation skills is a plausible expectation (Mann, Shakeshaft, Becker, & Kottkamp, 1999). The issue becomes much more complex when a teacher, school, or district is considering implementing a technology-supported innovation with a different kind of learning goal. Even if the program involves reading or mathematics, it may not call upon or teach the same kinds of skills or knowledge as the standardized tests used in a state's accountability system.

EXAMPLE OF AN INNOVATIVE PROGRAM

The SimCalc program, developed by researchers at the University of Massachusetts at Dartmouth and at SRI's Center for Technology in Learning can be used to illustrate this assessment dilemma. The rationale behind SimCalc's design is that important, but conceptually difficult mathematics content, can be taught to a broader range of students and at earlier ages through the judicious use of technology supports for graphic representation and modeling of abstract concepts, and the provision of a rich practice environment. More specifically, SimCalc focuses on teaching the mathematics of change and variation—the essence of calculus. The concept of rate of change is an essential part of mathematics, many branches of science, and practical decision making around areas such as deficit spending, economic growth, and personal finances. Even so, rates, accumulations, and velocity functions receive little coverage in middle school textbooks. SimCalc seeks to help middle school students understand these concepts by providing situations where rate varies, and where students can see how velocity functions relate to position functions (Roschelle, Pea, Hoadley, Gordin, & Means, 2000).

The original SimCalc software ran on computers costing $5,000 per student, but newer versions of the software run on a graphing calculator that costs less than $100 per student—an important consideration given the program's target audience of low-income, urban middle schoolers.

Although the efficacy of the SimCalc program has yet to be tested in a large-scale, rigorous evaluation, formative research conducted as part of the program's refinement efforts have documented, through video analysis of students as they reason through problems and through pre- and posttests on assessments of the mathematics-of-change concepts, that low-income middle school students do indeed improve markedly and in fact come to outperform college students who have not had the SimCalc program. This research (and the large-scale implementation and evaluation now getting underway) has required the development of an assessment of mathematics-of-change concepts. Although states assess middle school students' mathematics knowledge and skills, the standardized tests strive for broad coverage of the math content standards adopted by the states. As described above, concepts of velocity and rates of change receive little coverage in middle school curriculum or standards, and hence typically are not assessed in middle school standardized mathematics tests. If scores on a state mathematics achievement test were the only basis on which the effectiveness of the SimCalc program were evaluated, it would be almost sure to show no or very limited effects. Even the most rigorous experimental design cannot reveal true effects if the outcome measure is irrelevant or poorly aligned with the content that students are learning.

BROADER IMPLICATIONS

Given the NCLB requirement that schools demonstrate adequate yearly progress (AYP) on reading and mathematics test scores, states may be tempted to use the same test data to assess students' progress related to technology implementation. The discussion above, however, suggests that what appears to be the path of least resistance (i.e., using the same reading and mathematics test scores to report AYP progress on NCLB and to demonstrate the effects of the technology innovation) may in fact be strewn with land mines. The kinds of mathematical thinking supported by SimCalc are unlikely to be assessed on the state-mandated tests given to middle school students. Impact of the SimCalc experience on measures of mathematical skills not included in the SimCalc curriculum is likely to be weak or nonexistent. Use of an inappropriate measure of student learning could easily lead to an incorrect inference that a technology-based intervention is ineffective.

A decision maker considering making a major investment in a technology-based program would do well to carefully examine the nature of the program and its intended learning outcomes and to either identify existing, specialized assessments that tap those outcomes or devise a plan for their development. We will not know whether technology-based instructional programs are producing the intended student learning unless we assess these outcomes using instruments that are clearly aligned with the program content and that provide evidence of validity and reliability. This situation leads us to the conclusion that if the NCLB requirements are not to narrow the range of uses of technology in classrooms, there will be great need for techniques for the rigorous assessment of a wider range of content and skills than is found in most state accountability systems. Both a new technology for developing valid, reliable assessments of the kind of content and skills targeted by learning technologies, and ways to measure the more complex performances will be needed.

While many of the authors writing for *Evaluating Educational Technology* discuss the issue of obtaining appropriate student learning measures for evaluating learning technologies, two chapters have this issue as their central focus.

A PROJECT-BASED ASSESSMENT MODEL

In their chapter, "A Project-Based Approach to Assessing Technology," Henry J. Becker and Barbara E. Lovitts (2003) explore the concept of a "fair test" comparing students with and without experience using technology to do their schoolwork. They point out that by design, instruments used in standardized testing situations are largely composed of tasks for which computer experience is not likely to have made a difference. Becker and Lovitts argue that by having a limited range of tasks and employing a minimum-resource standardized testing environment that does not make use of technology, the tests that policymakers and the public pay attention to deny computer-capable students the opportunity to demonstrate what they can do *with* technology—an important competency in our Information Age. On the other hand, innovative technology-exploiting curriculum development projects often define assessment tasks that require technology-specific competencies (e.g., spreadsheet proficiency), thereby rendering comparisons between students with and without computer experiences hardly relevant. This approach fails to satisfy policymakers and a skeptical public who want comparative data.

Becker and Lovitts focus their chapter on competencies that could be acquired *without* use of computer resources or tools, but for which computer approaches may be advantageous. These competencies include:

- Students' levels of understanding in the academic subjects of the school curriculum, their ability to gain further understanding in these areas, and their ability to apply what they know in practical ways
- Students' capacities to undertake a wide variety of tasks in various work, citizen, and community roles that involve skills such as acquiring, evaluating, and using information, and skills of working in groups to solve problems and accomplish tasks

Becker and Lovitts propose both an assessment approach and a research design that involve defining outcome competencies and skills at a level of abstraction that permits computers to be used but does not require them to be used.

Becker and Lovitts propose the use of extended-in-time projects, in which participating teachers and researchers negotiate the boundaries for subject-matter content, component tasks and products, and ground rules to assure that the assessment activity supports each teacher's instructional objectives, and meets standards needed by researchers for comparability, validity, and reliability.

Their chapter outlines how this process might work in a matched design study in which technology use and teacher pedagogical approach are systematically varied while other factors—subject, grade level, ability level, school context—are held constant as far as possible. The assessment scoring would be set forth in a rubric that could be applied to all the projects—both those generated with computer supports and those generated without them. Scores on projects addressing the same content would be compared to each other, and meta-analytic techniques would be used to combine findings across sets of projects on different topics.

LEVERAGE POINTS FOR IMPROVING EDUCATIONAL ASSESSMENT

In their chapter, "Improving Educational Assessment," Robert J. Mislevy, Linda S. Steinberg, Russell G. Almond, Geneva D. Haertel, and William R. Penuel consider the issue of how advances in cognitive psychology, psychometrics, and technology itself can provide levers for developing the kinds of assessments of complex cognitive performances needed in evaluations of many learning technologies.

Advances in cognitive psychology deepen our understanding of how students gain and use knowledge. Advances in technology make it possible to capture more complex performances in assessment settings, by including, for example, simulation, interactivity, collaboration, and constructed responses. The challenge is in knowing just how to put this new knowledge to work.

Mislevy and his colleagues first review an evidence-centered framework for designing and analyzing assessments and then use this framework to discuss and to illustrate how advances in technology and in education and psychology can be harnessed to improve educational assessment.

The chapter is based on two premises: first, that the principles of evidentiary reasoning that underlie familiar assessments are a special case of more general principles; and second, that these principles can help educators design and analyze new kinds of technology-supported assessments, with new kinds of data, to serve new purposes. Technology-based assessments, developed using this approach, can provide good measures of complex performances that tap deeper understandings than can typically be assessed using traditional standardized achievement tests.

The evidence-centered approach is illustrated using examples from three examinations: (1) a familiar standardized test, the Graduate Record Examination (GRE); (2) a prototype simulation-based assessment of problem solving in dental hygiene for the Dental Interactive Simulations Corporation (DISC); and (3) an on-line performance task, the

MashpeeQuest, designed to evaluate students' information analysis skills, as part of Classroom Connect's AmericaQuest instructional program. A student, evidence, and task model are described for each of the three illustrative assessments.

To formulate a student model, the assessment designer must identify the complex of knowledge, skills, or other attributes that are to be assessed. To formulate the evidence model, the assessment designer must identify the behaviors or performances that should reveal the knowledge, skills, and attributes specified in the student model, and the connections among these performances. To formulate the task model, the assessment designer specifies the particular tasks or situations that will elicit the performances.

Using this evidence-based approach to assessment design, principled assessments can be developed that can be wedded with advances in psychology and technology. Technology, in particular, provides test developers certain advantages, including dynamic assembly of the student model; realistic presentation of problem tasks that can elicit direct evidence of desired student performances; automatic extraction and evaluation of key features of complex work products; and automatic assistance in item and task construction, presentation, and management. Using such tools, developers would be better equipped to develop assessments of the kinds of complex cognitive performances many learning technology developers hope to enhance.

CONCLUSION

Both sets of researchers featured in this section argue for the need to be able to assess more complex performances than are captured in the multiple-choice formats used on most standardized tests. Becker and Lovitts consider this assessment problem in the context of trying to design an evaluation that could be implemented in a statistically adequate sample of classrooms. One of their core ideas is that the assessment process must be integrated with the locally enacted curriculum in order to gain teacher cooperation. Their approach in effect would produce an assessment rubric for student projects that researchers could apply to projects developed with or without technology supports in much the same way that scoring rubrics are used to score student essays in large-scale writing assessments. With this approach, teachers whose classes are in a study do not need to devote class time to an external assessment since the students' projects function both as learning experiences and to produce an artifact that can be assessed.

Bob Mislevy and his colleagues do not take up the issue of evaluation design, but rather focus on the process of developing high-quality assessments of complex intellectual performances. Their analysis points to the detailed, careful analysis that should be the foundation for assessment development. They look to technology to help support the development of new kinds of assessments that may in turn be used to evaluate the learning effects of technology in classrooms. They argue that technology can be used to design, deliver, present, and score more complex assessment tasks than have typically been available.

An external perspective on the arguments raised by Becker and Lovitts and Mislevy et al. is provided by James Pellegrino, professor of education and psychology at the University of Illinois–Chicago.

Designs for Research on Technology and Assessment: Conflicting or Complementary Agendas?

James W. Pellegrino

Within the next decade, extremely powerful information and communication technologies will become ubiquitous in educational settings. They are almost certain to provoke fundamental changes in learning environments at all levels. Indeed, some of these changes are already occurring, enabling us to conjecture about their consequences for children, teachers, policymakers, and the public. Other applications of technology are beyond our speculative capacity. A decade ago, how many people could predict the sweeping effects of the Internet on education and other segments of society? Thus research on technology in education consists of reasoned guesses about profitable directions of inquiry and important questions worth asking.

One major change in education already underway is the influence of technology on what gets taught and how it is taught. Examples include the teaching of advanced thinking and reasoning skills within a discipline through the use of technology-mediated long-term inquiry projects. Such projects often integrate content and learning across disciplines. These technology-enhanced learning environments change the nature of what is to be learned and assessed. In some cases they have also become prototypes for the design and use of innovative technology-based tools and methods to support, scaffold, and assess student learning.

We are now faced with a number of challenges related to technology integration in education when it comes to matters of educational assessment. Unfortunately, the intellectual domains of educational technology and educational assessment are commonly viewed as largely separate if not conflicting enterprises. In many cases the practices pursued within each domain of activity seem to emanate from different perspectives about the nature of thinking and learning. For example, much of the contemporary work on technology integration in educational settings focuses on going beyond the accrual of factual knowledge, with an emphasis instead on teaching and learning for deep understanding within a domain. In contrast, much of current educational assessment focuses on surveying limited elements of domain knowledge, using standardized tasks that "drop-in-from-the-sky" to serve external accountability purposes. Thus it is not unusual for individuals working in the area of educational technology to regard typical educational assessment practices with serious disdain and as having little direct relevance to their educational objectives.

Is it possible to bring these two worlds of disciplined inquiry together, in ways that are productive for both educational practice and policy purposes? In *Evaluating Educational Technology* the chapters by Henry Jay Becker and Barbara E. Lovitts ("A Project-Based Approach to Assessing Technology") and Robert J. Mislevy, Linda S. Steinberg, Russell G. Almond, Geneva D. Haertel, and William Penuel ("Improving Educational Assessment") consider several major issues and take very different approaches regarding some possibilities for merging these two worlds. For Becker and Lovitts, the central question is how we bypass many existing assessment problems in pursuit of designs that can yield strong data about the effects of educational technology. They are seeking answers to important policy-relevant questions regarding the impact of technology on valued educational outcomes. For Mislevy et al., the central question is how to capitalize on various intellectual developments in the cognitive and measurement sciences, as well as information technologies, to design assessments that answer important questions about what students know. Their agenda is research and development on better assessment practices that can be used to serve a variety of purposes. Among these is the general program evaluation purpose in Becker and Lovitts's proposed research design, as well as assessment of learning outcomes within technology-enhanced instructional settings.

These are two very interesting and complex chapters. Both contain a wealth of information and each has a complex argument structure. Connecting these two very different works together is a challenge for many reasons, not the least of which is that they are attempting to solve two very different problems. Nonetheless, it is important to seek out the important messages within each, consider the differences in what they conclude about directions for research, and see if there are ways in which they intersect. The overall goal of their work and this volume is to help frame a research agenda on technology focused on answering important questions about learning and teaching.

COMMENTS ON A PROJECT-BASED APPROACH TO TECHNOLOGY ASSESSMENT

The central issue in Becker and Lovitts's chapter is the problem of obtaining information about the effects of information technology on valued educational outcomes, in ways that fairly contrast technology-enhanced learning environments with those lacking such an emphasis. The Becker and Lovitts chapter is not about assessment per se even though a substantial part of what they discuss concerns educational assessment. Rather, the focus is on the collection of assessment information that serves the purpose of evaluating and contrasting program outcomes.

Becker and Lovitts cover multiple topics in educational assessment such as the limitations of using standardized achievement tests for program evaluation studies, as well as concerns with using alternatives such as performance assessments. Many of the points raised about the limitations of various types of assessment practices are quite valid. This is also true of their discussion of the limitations of research conducted to date on technology-based educational programs. The examples provided show the difficulty of establishing an empirical knowledge base that explains and justifies the benefits of using technology in education. They do a very convincing job of showing that there are many problems in answering a policy-relevant question of great importance, "Does technology make a difference and how much of a difference does it make?" Not the least of the problems is the assessment dilemma—"What is sensible to assess and how can we do so in ways that aren't confounded with technology experience and use?" While the question is simple, seeking answers is anything but simple.

The proposed solution is a contrastive design with multiple teachers and classrooms where the critical outcome is performance in a relatively extended project-based task. The final task product is held constant across selected sets of sites. These and other features of the situation—such as the content domain, rubrics for judging the final products, and other related issues—are negotiated and mutually agreed to ahead of time. Doing so permits control of a great many critical variables that could otherwise influence the outcome. In contrast, the central variable of how students acquire the critical knowledge and skills needed to address the project-based task is left open to different implementations. In one set of implementations, technology is presumably a primary way by which children acquire the target knowledge and skills that they use to complete the project-based task.

In the contrasting set of implementations there is no specific use of technology to accomplish the learning goals. The design they propose includes elements of a matrix-sampling approach as typically applied to large-scale program evaluation studies. Across sites, different subsets of "experimental" and "control" group children would work on different project-based tasks. In such designs, the data of individual students is less of a concern than the aggregated data across multiple, matched samples of students. While the generalized two groups evaluation design described by Becker and Lovitts has various complexities, it ostensibly could be pulled off.

One has to question, however, the cost of executing such a complex contrastive design relative to its prospective benefits. If one invested in such a study, how much in the way of detailed, policy-relevant information would we have at the end? Just how large an effect size would be convincing, and for what audience? There is also the issue of pursuing a design that hinges on using one project-based task versus designs considering performance on multiple tasks. It is not clear how many tasks and task variations should be used in the proposed evaluation plan. Answers to these and other critical questions about the Becker and Lovitts design depend on two broader concerns.

The first concern is what is the most productive way to view the role of technology in enhancing learning and teaching—as a general and relatively undifferentiated entity or as a set of specific tools designed to selectively enhance different features of learning environments. The Becker and Lovitts approach is focused on the undifferentiated technology model, which some might argue is a questionable emphasis. Greater consideration of this issue will be provided later in this commentary. The second concern involves the quality of the assessment tasks in the Becker and Lovitts evaluation design, as defined by how they map against a model of the underlying knowledge and competencies to be assessed. In reality, the value of the data derived from the approach proposed by Becker and Lovitts depends on carefully thinking through many of the assessment issues considered by Mislevy et al.

COMMENTS ON PRINCIPLED ASSESSMENT DESIGN

The chapter by Mislevy and his colleagues presents a complex set of ideas on the nature of educational assessment, including how it should be connected to advances in cognitive psychology, psychometrics, and technology. A set of three examples are repeated and developed throughout the paper to make the constructs more concrete. Even so, readers will need to think very carefully about all the elements of the authors' arguments and how the pieces of this generalized approach to assessment fit together. The central idea is that assessment should be conceived as a process of reasoning from evidence. This process includes three components: a student model, an observations model, and an evidence or interpretation model. They show how these three elements of the evidentiary reasoning logic can be applied to examples that range from the GRE, a very constrained assessment setting with a limited student model, to more open-ended assessment settings with very broad student model constructs, such as inquiry tasks embedded within technology delivery systems.

The authors argue that we can do a much better job across a variety of assessment contexts (1) by capitalizing on advances in cognitive theory and statistics and (2) tailoring our assessments to the job of providing information and evidence that fits our particular assessment purpose. The GRE, DISC, and MashpeeQuest assessment examples are elaborated to illustrate key concepts such as what might be contained within the student model, what constitutes the interpretive or evidence model, and what needs to be part of the observations or task model. Of particular concern is how the three models interact within the broader reasoning-from-evidence framework.

In contrast to the Becker and Lovitts chapter, Mislevy et al. is focused explicitly on issues of assessment design rather than application per se. It is not about assessing technology's impact on learning but ways to think about how technology can facilitate the assessment process. The impact of technology on assessment potentially comes in many forms including (1) assisting in the process of accumulating evidence to support a student model, for example by presenting tasks germane to this process and keeping track of responses, and (2) handling some of the statistical complexity associated with making inferences from observations related to complex cognitive models of student knowledge and skills.

POINTS OF CONVERGENCE

The general ideas and specific examples in the Mislevy et al. chapter can be used to consider several of the assessment issues related to technology discussed by Becker and Lovitts. For example, we can understand the problem of using typical standardized tests to evaluate the effects of many technology-based instructional programs, especially those with an emphasis on learning *with* technology, as instances of a poor fit between the observations model and the student model. Typical standardized test tasks provide observations aligned with a student model that focuses on specific types of declarative and procedural knowledge that may or may not have been acquired with the assistance of technology-based programs. Thus it should come as no surprise that there is often a perceived mismatch between educational technology programs and data obtained from standardized tests. Yet many persist in using such data as a basis for judging the effectiveness and value of investments in educational technology.

Assessing the knowledge that students acquire in specific technology-based learning environments where the learning is mediated by interaction *with* the technology requires tasks and observations designed to provide evidence consistent with an appropriate student model. The latter identifies the specific knowledge and skills that students are expected to learn and the precise form of that knowledge, including what aspects of it are tied to specific technology tools. This process of matching the observations model to the student model is very similar to what has been done within the Development-Linked Research category described by Becker and Lovitts.

The AmericaQuest program and MashpeeQuest assessment example in Mislevy et al. serve to illustrate how we might conceptualize assessing the impact of technology on valued educational outcomes that transcend technology-based learning environments. MashpeeQuest is an on-line performance task designed to evaluate the AmericaQuest instructional program. AmericaQuest aids students in developing persuasive arguments supported by evidence from the course's web site in their own research. For this complex learning environment Mislevy et al. define various appropriate student model constructs like information analysis skills and problem-solving skills which can be further broken out at varying levels of detail and grain size.

For assessment of student learning in AmericaQuest, tasks like MashpeeQuest are designed because they elicit complex sets of observations appropriate to the student model knowledge variables. The observations can be mapped against a set of evidence rules tied to the multiple elements of the student model. Such an assessment approach serves two critical assessment purposes very well. The first is a formative purpose in which the assessment goal is to obtain information to assist further learning by students using the AmericaQuest environment. Performance on a task like MashpeeQuest would tell teachers what students know in ways that were diagnostic and potentially prescriptive for further work in the AmericaQuest environment. The second is a summative purpose in which the goal is to determine how much of the intended knowledge and competencies had been achieved after students had completed using the AmericaQuest program for some fixed period of time.

Consider instead that our interest is the comparative evaluation design proposed by Becker and Lovitts. Ostensibly, the AmericaQuest environment is designed to develop important inquiry and problem-solving skills that extend beyond the Web-based world of information sources that students explore when using this technology system. It could conceivably be a way in which students might address an extended project-based task of the type that Becker and Lovitts propose using in their general design. Thus many elements of the student model for AmericaQuest would seem to fit the broader evaluation design. Given that this is the case, would a non-technology version of the MashpeeQuest task also serve as a fair test of learning for students who did and did not have access to the AmericaQuest environment? Perhaps, but it would need substantial changes; and what information would be lost in the process? How would some other project-based task work, and would it be a fair test? Answers to these and other critical questions are not easy to come by unless we get very specific about all three elements of the Mislevy et al. evidentiary reasoning approach.

A careful consideration of the Mislevy et al. arguments shows that successful execution of the type of evaluation design proposed by Becker and Lovitts is no simple task. We need a very careful analysis of the skills and knowledge we wish to assess—the student model; we need a clear sense of how the tasks to be used would elicit those skills and knowledge—the observations model; and we need a way to fit the student model and the observations together—the interpretive model. The Mislevy et al. evidentiary reasoning scheme helps define what to assess and how to assess it, especially at a level of specificity that allows the Becker and Lovitts design to work.

SOME FINAL THOUGHTS ABOUT RESEARCH DIRECTIONS

The proposals offered by Becker and Lovitts and Mislevy et al., for research related to technology, assessment, and student learning imply a very extensive program of work. As argued above, the two approaches to framing important research issues share overlapping constructs and can be brought together in fruitful ways. One thing that needs to be considered is how we think about the role of information and communication technologies in educational settings. There are multiple elements of powerful learning environments that are differentially enabled by various technologies. Some focus on the knowledge to be learned. Others focus on the learner's current state of knowledge and providing assistance with understanding concepts. Still others focus on making the student's thinking visible or on the process of knowledge sharing and community building. Thus it may be fruitful in designing evaluation and assessment studies to plan for a diversified approach to asking questions about learning in technology-enhanced environments rather than treating technology as a general and relatively undifferentiated treatment.

For multiple reasons, we need to consider the use of a portfolio of studies focused on how technology supports the acquisition of various types of knowledge and cognitive skills, with appropriate accompanying assessments. Such a plan would consider the effectiveness of various technology-based systems and tools for supporting specific and general aspects of student learning. The Becker and Lovitts design is one instance of a larger class of studies that will ultimately need to differentiate among various instructional approaches and technologies and how they are used in different classrooms. For example, in the Becker and Lovitts design we might expect large classroom variation in the effects of technology on project-based task performance with the result that effect sizes in general purpose evaluation designs could be small unless there is a way to isolate technology implementation variables at a more fine-grained level. Thus a complementary approach to consider in designing an overall program of research is to plan ahead to systematically accumulate evidence over multiple studies so that meta-analytic methods for data synthesis can be used to examine patterns of effect sizes and thereby selectively address important policy and practice questions.

Finally, we need to consider the fact that we may never know how big an effect size is policy relevant, especially in a world where it is often difficult to precisely specify cost-benefit trade-offs. Even if large and replicable effects are obtained, of a size convincing to members of the educational policy and practice community, we should still want to know what they mean, and why they occurred. This is why assessment scenarios must be designed in which considerable care has been given to specifying the student model competencies we wish to assess, the evidence model tied to those competencies, including evidence embedded within technology-based worlds and evidence not biased by technology use, and the tasks that will yield the evidence we need. While much remains to be done, it is time to move beyond a perspective that research on technology in education is at odds with practical matters of assessment. Instead, we need to recognize technology's affordances for pursuing a richer approach to assessment. The latter permits asking and answering questions about learning and teaching of considerable relevance for advancing theory, practice, and educational policy.

PART III

LOOKING AT EFFECTS OVER THE LONG TERM

In contrast to other countries, the United States has a strong tradition of state and local control of education. Without a national curriculum or testing system, the decision about what and how to teach devolves to decisionmakers at the state, district, school, and classroom levels. The American educational system is thus characterized both by multiple levels and by complexity. A student's experience of educational technology is likely to be a product of at least five influences:

- State or district decisions concerning investment levels and allocation formulas for technology infrastructure
- State assessment and accountability requirements
- District curriculum guidelines and instructional materials purchasing decisions
- School interest in promoting and supporting technology use across the curriculum
- Individual teachers' choice of software and interest in and skill in incorporating that software into their instructional repertoires

Within a given classroom, the students' technology experiences are perhaps most influenced by the teacher's decision to incorporate specific pieces of software (say *Accelerated Reader* or *Geometer's Sketchpad*), technology tools (Internet search engines, word processing), or resources (the National Geographic Web site activities or the American Memory Project collection of Civil War artifacts) into his or her teaching. We might want to study the implementation or evaluate the effectiveness of that particular piece of software, tool, or resource, as discussed in the first section of this volume. Results of such research could inform the teacher's future practice or even the decision of whether to use that piece of software with the next class.

At the same time, use of the software or resource requires the presence of hardware, wiring, and technical support. These infrastructure resources are typically paid for at the district or state level (or with the state and district acting as distributors of federal funds). While the teacher cannot use *Accelerated Reader* if the needed technology infrastructure is lacking, the technology infrastructure, especially to the extent that it involves both internal and external networks, is almost never purchased with the idea of supporting just a single application. Hence the district administrator, school board, or state legislature that decides to invest in high-speed Internet connections for every high school has in mind a broader set of goals than enabling the use of *Geometer's Sketchpad* or the National Geographic Web site. Those who invest in the educational technology infrastructure are seeking more than just demonstrable improvements on a narrow piece of the curriculum. Investors want to enable use of a multitude of technology tools and software programs across the curriculum and across grade levels. They hope to see not just measurable improvements from a single piece of software in a single subject in a single grade but broad, long-term benefits of using technology in schools that impact many curricular areas at all grade levels. These benefits presumably are associated with students having multiple technology experiences over time that will influence important student outcomes, although the effects may not show up for some time. The types of outcomes that might be influenced include analytic thinking, a strong academic self-concept, a pattern of taking rigorous courses, and decisions about pursuing higher education and productive careers. Because the time frame to achieve these outcomes is so long and the stakes so high, few districts are likely to be willing to comply with a random-assignment protocol involving rich technology versus no school access to technology over a large segment of students' education. How then can it be determined whether the costly investment required to create a school or district technology infrastructure is worth the effort?

In this section of the book we deal with research design guidance from groups interested in tackling this thorny issue. In *Evaluating Educational Technology*, they promote two key features of research designs involving:

- Assessment of influences at multiple levels of the education system (i.e., features of the classroom, school, and district)
- Collection of data from the same groups (of students, teachers, or schools) on multiple occasions over an extended period of time (i.e. longitudinal designs)

CONSIDERING EDUCATIONAL TECHNOLOGY AS A
MULTILEVEL PHENOMENON

In his chapter, "The Advantages of Longitudinal Design," Russell Rumberger of the University of California, Santa Barbara, presents a conceptual framework for evaluating technology as a multilevel phenomenon with factors at the school, classroom, and student levels that can impact student learning. This multilevel characterization is not unique to educational technology. Similar frameworks have been used in prior research to study other types of inputs, processes, and outcomes of schooling. Rumberger's framework recognizes that educational technology encompasses a vast array of hardware and software that can be used for a wide variety of educational purposes, from the very specific to the very general. Moreover, these technologies can be located in different levels of the educational system and used by different people. For example, all of a school's teachers may have desktop computers linked to an intranet that enables them to share information and instructional resources. District databases may be accessible by school administrators, teachers, or parents. The school may have one or more computer labs available to any class whose teacher signs up. Some classrooms may be equipped with Internet access and powerful computers while others are not. Teachers may make individual choices to use specific on-line resources with their students.

Rumberger's framework suggests that to properly evaluate the impact of an educational technology, one must not only specify the nature of the technology to be evaluated but also the level at which it typically operates. Conceptualizing educational technology as a multilevel phenomenon permits evaluators to overcome some of the difficulties of designing credible evaluations of educational technology. The framework is also useful for examining the impact of educational technologies over both the short and the long terms. While the concepts and measures specified in the framework are not tied to any particular time frame, evaluating the impact of educational technologies on student learning and achievement over time would require measuring change in the inputs and processes over the same period of time.

Rumberger articulates several difficulties that frequently are encountered in evaluating technology:

- Identifying or developing appropriate outcome measures that can be used to document the effects of particular technologies (e.g., general word processors, simulations based on constructivist models of learning and teaching)

- Providing sufficient professional development so that teachers can maintain the fidelity of the technology intervention in a school- or field-based setting
- Determining whether the evaluative research should be conducted in a small versus large number of research sites (A small-scale study would be less expensive and would be likely to have greater fidelity in the technology implementation; a large-scale study conducted in more sites would provide a stronger base for judging the effectiveness of the technology and represent more of the types of educational settings that use the technology, but at the cost of less control over the fidelity of the implementation.)
- Determining the trade-offs among the advantages and disadvantages of alternative potential research designs
- Selecting appropriate control groups for which critical features of classroom practice, along with the specific uses of educational technologies, can be varied and accurately documented in order to understand exactly what is being changed
- Determining whether the study will be of short or long duration (Short-term studies may be useful in examining the impact of a more narrowly focused form of educational technology, such as software for teaching a particular curriculum unit; long-term studies may be needed to look at the cumulative impacts of a more general form of technology, such as the Internet, that could be used for many different educational activities and whose benefits could be expected to accrue over a long period of time.)

Evaluations based on Rumberger's framework would do several things:

- Investigate technology within multiple contexts of family, school, and classroom
- Employ a sampling framework to insure substantial variability in learning contexts
- Focus on learning or the growth in appropriate learning measures over time
- Collect data at multiple points in the learning process
- Employ suitable multilevel modeling techniques (e.g., hierarchical linear modeling) in order to correctly identify the impact of technology at different levels

Rumberger believes that evaluations based on this framework could be done using experimental or survey research designs. However, experimental designs are more compatible with evaluations of specific, relatively short-term technology implementations while survey-based designs can be implemented more readily over long time periods in studies of the cumulative impacts of general technology support.

MEASURING THE IMPLEMENTATION AND IMPACT OF TECHNOLOGY

In their chapter, "Studies of Technology Implementation and Effects," Larry V. Hedges, Spyros Konstantopoulos, and Amy Thoreson of the University of Chicago, make the argument that no single study or even single type of study will be adequate for understanding and monitoring the implementation and effects of educational technology. Instead, they propose a system of data collection, including studies of different types for different purposes. They argue that surveys, randomized experiments, and longitudinal designs are all needed in order to capture needed information on technology use and effects.

A comprehensive program of evaluative research to systematically examine the effects of technology should include a program of interrelated studies. The individual component studies would focus on different aspects of technology, use different methods, and have different purposes and time horizons. Some of the components (such as the large-scale survey component included in the National Assessment of Educational Progress) are either already in place or could be put in place by modifying ongoing data collections slightly to include information concerning technology use. Other components would have to be created as wholly new systems. In any case, the authors believe that regarding these various research pieces all as components of a unified system could bring certain efficiencies and improve the overall quality of information about technology in education.

Hedges et al. provide specific recommendations regarding the use of surveys to assess technology use and effects. To measure the implementation of technology, large-scale surveys of representative samples of American classrooms are needed. The National Assessment of Educational Progress (NAEP), which has conducted both general-purpose and targeted surveys, provides some idea of the potential of surveys for assessing technology—especially the value of targeted surveys. Hedges and his colleagues point out the advantages of considering all NAEP surveys as components of a single data collection. Even so, assessment of the impact of technology on the basis of cross-sectional surveys (where comparisons are made across different groups of students measured at a single point in time) is difficult, as illustrated by analyses of NAEP data on technology use and achievement. This chapter argues that cross-sectional surveys alone (in which schools or classrooms with differing amounts of technology access or use are compared in terms of student achievement) simply cannot be used to make persuasive causal arguments about technology's effects. Despite statistical attempts to control for differences other than those of technology use, it is always possible that other differences between the schools or classes cause those who happen to use technology more frequently or in different ways to also produce higher achievement scores.

Hedges et al. propose that such survey data be supplemented with intensive studies of technology use in classrooms. Longitudinal studies (in which the same students, classrooms or schools are measured at multiple points over time) can provide much less ambiguous evidence about cause than can cross-sectional studies. If the same students, teachers, or schools are measured at multiple points and improvements are observed after the introduction of technology, many potential alternative explanations of the improvement can be ruled out (e.g., it is not because the students with technology were smarter or came from more enriched home environments, since they are the same as the "low-technology" students measured before the technology innovation). The measurement of implementation processes within classes and schools can also be an important benefit of such studies. However, even longitudinal studies do not rule out all rival hypotheses about cause if they do not incorporate random assignment. The authors agree that randomized experiments provide the least ambiguous information about causal effects, and argue that they should be seriously considered as part of a system of work to understand the effects of educational technology.

A major consideration in designing an evaluative research program focused on technology use and effects is how quickly technology and technological competence is changing. Such change has the potential to make information generated by any single study rapidly obsolete. Consequently, a major concern is how to develop information on the effects of technology in a timely fashion that incorporates results of multiple studies. New strategies may be needed, and "indicator" measures may need to be developed to delineate trends in technology for purposes of policy formation.

Hedges et al. suggest establishing a system of teacher-researchers in a network of schools distributed across the country. The purpose of the network would be to provide ongoing feedback about technology issues. In principle, the system would alert educators and policymakers to emerging trends that were not anticipated. The network could be adaptive in the sense that it could be used not only to identify new data needs but also to collect preliminary data about emerging issues. Moreover, such a network of teacher-researchers could provide useful formative information for the design of surveys or other, more intensive data collections at a later time.

STUDYING THE BROAD IMPACTS OF EDUCATIONAL TECHNOLOGY OVER TIME

In their chapter, "Studying the Cumulative Impacts of Educational Technology," Barbara Means, Mary Wagner, Geneva D. Haertel, and Harold S. Javitz of SRI International outline a design for a national longitudinal study of the impact of learning technology use. Following a nationally representative cohort of students from ninth grade through the end of secondary school, this longitudinal study of educational technology would collect data on the nature and quantity of students' technology use and outcomes, such as school attendance and engagement, self-concept as a learner, technology skills, career and college plans, achievement test performance, and scores on performance tests that target advanced information synthesis and communication skills. Within the context of this broad longitudinal study of students' use of technology in and out of school, focused studies would explore the implementation and impact of technology use in specific classrooms. Both the focused classroom studies and the broader longitudinal study would incorporate a common core of data elements.

With the student as the primary unit of analysis, the longitudinal study described by Means et al. would employ a large enough sample to enable examination of a wide variety of experiences for key subgroups of students. The authors suggest that such a study would be most informative if it included both a large, national probability sample and a special sample of students clustered in classrooms whose technology use practices are studied intensively and, in some cases, manipulated through carefully designed experiments. This would insure inclusion of students with extensive technology experiences of different types, permit the investigation of causal questions, and support extrapolations of trends in a world where the amount and nature of technology access and use are changing rapidly.

Means et al. discuss the sampling plan and parameters needed to satisfy the study's multiple purposes. They propose a two-stage sampling plan that would be used to draw (1) a stratified random sample of local education agencies (LEAs) that represent several major sources of variations (i.e., district size, region, district/community wealth, technology infrastructure) and (2) a representative student sample (i.e., a random sample of ninth-grade students selected within each sampled LEA, with all ninth-grade students within an LEA having an equal probability of selection). This approach would ensure variability in key student factors—such as gender, ethnicity, and other demographics—as well as family factors—such as parent involvement in, and support of, educational activities—that are important influences on student achievement.

Repeated measurements would assess changes in students' in-school and out-of-school uses of technology and their outcomes in a variety of domains as students move from ninth grade through graduation from secondary school. The power of longitudinal research is that repeated measurements of the same individuals over time allows for an assessment of change that is not possible with other designs. As additional data points become available, it would be possible to compute growth curves for individual students and groups of students. It is likely that profiles of growth would differ for the various subgroups of students. In addition, analyses undoubtedly would reveal change in different degrees or even in different directions across the multiple dimensions of technology use and the multiple student outcomes of interest. Although it would be valuable to look at the change or growth in any single dimension of technology use or student outcomes, a key benefit of such a study would be to examine the multidimensionality and relationships among the technology uses and student outcomes in order to capture a realistic picture of change in classrooms, schools, and LEAs over time.

The authors assert that a study of the scope and magnitude of a national longitudinal study of educational technology would require a comprehensive conceptual framework and set of research questions derived from a process that includes representatives of key stakeholder groups (such as state and district policymakers, practitioners, researchers, and public interest groups).

CONCLUSION

The multibillion-dollar annual investment in technology for America's schools is based on an implicit assumption that technology supports for learning will have broad, long-lasting impacts on students. Features and actions of multiple levels of the educational system will influence how technology is used and its effectiveness.

The chapters of *Evaluating Educational Technology* discussed in this part all present frameworks for taking the multiple levels of the education system into account in designing research on technology, and all view longitudinal studies as a complement to, rather than substitute for, other types of studies. Nevertheless, the dominant theme in these chapters is the need for analytic approaches that can handle the complexity of a multilevel intervention and for longitudinal research designs that measure inputs, processes, and effects at a minimum of two (and preferably more) points in time. Valerie Lee, professor of education at the University of Michigan, Ann Arbor, comments on these research proposals, highlighting unresolved technical issues and resource considerations.

Evaluating Educational Technology with Complex Designs

Valerie E. Lee

As technology use in schools has grown exponentially in the last decade, the importance of assessing its effects is both more and less important now than in the past. The increased importance stems from Americans' desire to know whether this huge public investment has recognized payoffs. As reasonable as this seems, I propose an alternative perspective: Technology may be one of many educational innovations in which our policymakers and the public they serve have so much faith that evaluating its efficacy is almost beside the point. Technology use across our society is exploding, so it seems reasonable that the nation's children need to use it wisely. Where better to learn how than in school? Why, then, should we need evaluations to make decisions of this magnitude?

The authors in the research volume have fully embraced the "more important" argument, seemingly drawing a parallel between investment in educational technology and needed investment in evaluating its efficacy. The authors of the chapters that address the subject of Part III of this book propose very ambitious plans for evaluating the effects of U.S. students' access to technology in their classrooms, their schools, and outside of school. The complexity of their designs reflects both the complexity of the phenomenon and the authors' skills in recognizing that complexity.

SPECIFIC DESIGNS

In their chapter, "Studies of Technology Implementation and Effects," Hedges, Konstantopoulos, and Thoreson suggest an evaluation design that encompasses four types of studies: (1) large-scale surveys describing the availability and use of educational technology (possibly an add-on to the National Assessment of Educational Progress); (2) intensive studies of how technology is used in schools and classrooms; (3) randomized and longitudinal studies designed to determine causal relationships between technology experience and use and outcomes; and (4) studies of technology usage and trends. The authors' proposed designs would use survey data (some longitudinal, some cross-sectional), observations in classrooms, experimental designs, and different types of outcomes measured on students and teachers.

Particularly useful is these authors' recognition that studies need to be responsive to the rapidly changing field of educational technology, so that designers and implementers receive information more quickly than what would be available from longitudinal studies. To get data rapidly, they suggest administering shorter surveys and structured interviews in field settings. Also interesting is their suggestion to develop a new group of school-based professionals: teacher-researchers, who would divide their responsibilities between teaching and studying practice in their schools (as part of studies of technology usage and trends). However, more detail is needed about the design of the four types of studies and the modes for data collection and analysis.

In his chapter, "The Advantages of Longitudinal Design," Rumberger's major contribution is his recognition of the multilevel nature of the educational enterprise and the need to design evaluations that reflect these levels. In a design that is more general and simpler than that proposed in the Lesgold chapter (see Part I of this volume), Rumberger's model of schooling is divided into three parts: (1) inputs, (2) the educational process itself, and (3) outputs (i.e., learning and achievement). Because students' learning occurs over time, as does the educational process students experience (as discussed in Parts II and III of this book), Rumberger argues that evaluations must be longitudinal as well as multilevel.

The design suggested here focuses on students between 9th and 12th grades, although Rumberger also alludes to longitudinal studies that could follow younger children (say, kindergarten through grade 3, grades 3 through 6, and grades 6 through 9). He recognizes that in order to evaluate instructional effects (exactly what technology evaluations typically would do), researchers need to take into account in their data analysis that students are clustered within classrooms, and classrooms within schools, as they learn and engage in educational experiences. This means that the statistical interdependencies among the student-, classroom-, and school-level data must be considered. (Typically, data from extant longitudinal data sets, such as those available through the National Center for Education Statistics, do not allow for the statistical interdependencies caused by the clustering of students within classrooms and schools). Thus the study Rumberger proposes employs a sampling design that does take into account the multilevel structure of the data to be collected, such that students are contained (or nested) in classrooms (he suggests 20 students per teacher), and classrooms are nested in schools. Rumberger sings the praises of multilevel modeling using hierarchical linear modeling (HLM) software to analyze data, both in terms of studying change or growth, and in terms of the multilevel structure of the data and phenomena being studied. However, he does not provide any details about how the classroom nesting level might be incorporated into a large design, as classrooms change every year.

In their chapter, "Studying the Cumulative Impacts of Educational Technology," Means, Wagner, Haertel, and Javitz propose a very detailed evaluation design, one that would be both descriptive and explanatory. Their study would include two phases: (1) a longitudinal study focused on a nationally representative sample of students and LEAs (i.e., school districts) and (2) a test bed of smaller studies, some experimental in nature, that focus more closely on particular educational technology innovations in particular classrooms. The samples for these two studies would be linked, presumably by focusing the test bed studies in the same school districts that would be part of the larger longitudinal study. These authors focus on evaluating technology in high schools, and they would follow a group of ninth graders through high school. They state quite clearly that they would analyze data from the longitudinal part of the study with the individual student as the unit of analysis. They propose an extensive set of outcomes: standardized tests, performance assessments, students' engagement in school, and educational plans and aspirations.

It is clear that these authors, all staff members of SRI, have much experience with educational technology and are very familiar with the issues involved in evaluating its effects. A major strength of this chapter is the depth of understanding of the phenomenon. Their two-phase design resembles the proposal by Hedges et al. and that of Lesgold, although Means et al. provide more detail about the two design phases. The authors mention using HLM for data analysis for the longitudinal phase, but it is unclear exactly how they would use the analytic technique (i.e., growth curve modeling or taking into account clustering or nesting of students in districts). It is unclear also how the classroom/teacher and school data would be incorporated into the analysis.

SOME COMMON THEMES

All these authors recognize the difficulty of evaluating the impact of educational technology on student learning, and all of them have proposed complex designs. Included in all of these authors' designs is the need to study students over time. Thus all have proposed longitudinal designs. To one degree or other, most of these studies also recognize the need for studying educational technology with more than one type of study. Hedges and his colleagues have proposed the widest variety of designs, recognizing that knowledge about access and usage are quite different from knowledge about impact.

Most authors acknowledge the value of smaller studies that focus more intensely on the efficacy of particular technologies. The authors' suggestions for how to carry out this type of study are quite different. There is also recognition, across the authors, of the need for multiple outcomes. Some authors provide more information than others about the measures they would use, but all suggest that technology might impact a wide range of outcomes.

SOME QUESTIONS ABOUT EVALUATING EDUCATIONAL TECHNOLOGY

Educational technology is not an area where my research is focused, but I have experience in evaluating educational effects on students, particularly using multilevel methods, large-scale nationally representative samples, and longitudinal designs. Thus I direct my final comments to a few general issues that seem relevant in the context of these chapters.

Are these proposals specific to technology?

I suggest that most of the ideas laid out in these evaluation plans are not restricted to educational technology, but are relevant for evaluating any educational intervention (or even more generally, any social program). A larger issue, one to which Lesgold alluded, is that educational innovations in general are evaluated either modestly or not at all. The public and practitioners are so anxious to flock to particular new ideas, and the government is so unwilling to invest the time, money, and patience in solid evaluations, that almost nothing gets evaluated properly. We really don't know whether many social or educational interventions have the effects their proponents argue that they do, even though the programs have been in place for years and years. Thus I suggest that we could substitute almost any innovation in place of technology here, and these excellent suggestions would still be valid. On the other hand, as I suggested at the outset, it could also be argued that we might not need to evaluate educational technology, as there are probably very few decisions that would be made on the basis of these evaluations (particularly the long-term ones).

What about the cost of such an evaluation?

If it were necessary to conduct complex evaluations to really learn what innovations in the field of educational technology work, what working means, and in what settings, then one might wonder why this wasn't done before the incredible scaling up that has taken place in the field of educational technology. Among the several reasons, let me suggest three. First, no one wants to wait that long for the answer to the "does it work" question (something Hedges et al. suggested). Second, there is no designated decision maker responsible for deciding when and where these studies should be done, or whether the money for these evaluations might be better spent evaluating something else (or even on another intervention). There is fierce competition for available funds for educational research and evaluation. Some might question whether such a huge investment should be targeted at educational technology when the efficacy of many other educational innovations has never been determined with complex designs and/or nationally representative samples. The third and probably primary reason is because the evaluation designs proposed here are extremely costly. I'm surprised that the authors either skirted or ignored this serious barrier.

On what outcomes should educational technology effects be assessed?

All authors mentioned achievement as the primary outcome. However, some mentioned the problem of using standardized tests to measure the higher order thinking and complex problem-solving strategies that are the expected outcomes from the newest educational technologies. Lesgold mentioned using assessments for the New Standards Project, Rumberger mentioned portfolios or performance assessments, and Means et al. also propose to measure more complex learning and problem-solving skills. However, these authors did not discuss the substantial problems in using these more authentic assessments to measure change over time, at their present stage of development, although most discussed problems with these measures' validity and reliability. To me, this presents a serious conundrum, in that the assessment tools most appropriate to evaluate the impacts of students' exposure to the best of educational technology—the treatments—don't match what educators hope will be the learning involved. I recognize that these authors cannot discuss every detail of these designs here. Nevertheless, how portfolios or performance assessments can be used to measure learning over time is a question that didn't receive much attention in these chapters. However, this could become a big problem in their evaluations. If it is difficult to measure the change generated by technology because measures have low reliability, then the effects of technology would be systematically underestimated on these outcomes—and, of course, these are the outcomes on which we might put most of our confidence.

How can we untangle educational technology from more general instruction?

Rumberger mentioned this problem, and I would like to underscore its importance. More and more, as educational technology has become integrated into the school curriculum, it is embedded within an instructional approach that is often called "constructivist," "student-centered," "authentic," "inquiry-based," or "interactive." One aspect of this problem is a standard evaluation issue: To what is the particular implementation of educational technology to be compared? Ideally, we would want another classroom that used the same type of teaching without using educational technology in the instruction. But do such places really exist? More generally, this becomes a measurement issue. How do you measure students' exposure to particular types of technology above and beyond their exposure to instruction, when one is almost completely embedded in the other? How can you be sure that any technology impact is not simply a function of the instructional approach used?

How do we measure change over time, and what is changing?

All the authors recognized that assessing long-term effects is important, and that learning itself is a longitudinal process. However, the actual design of schooling really makes assessing long-term change and how educational technology impacts learning quite difficult. Why? In most schools, students change teachers virtually every year, except in rare circumstances. Thus their exposure to any particular educational setting (with or without technology) is relatively short. The smaller scale studies described by these authors probably wouldn't suffer from this problem. One would look at one-year gains on achievement tests (or some other outcome), and match that with one-year exposure to particular technology settings. However, what if the effect were lagged (i.e., students might actually benefit from this exposure after they leave the classroom)? Over the longer term, what if the target students encountered other educational settings during subsequent years in the same school that might "undo" the effects from previous exposure?

To me, this seems to be an almost insolvable dilemma. Student learning is continuous and long-term, but exposure to any particular education intervention is usually short-term (a year at most, sometimes even shorter). Obviously, this is a problem in evaluating almost any instructional approach using longitudinal data gathered at several points in time. It might make sense to think of whole school technology interventions, ones that endure over several years in a student's life, and to make comparisons between schools that do and do not use particular technology interventions. However appealing and reasonable such a design might seem in analytic terms, I suspect that educational innovations in the field of technology are very rarely whole-school interventions. Even if they were, it is likely that students' actual exposure in different classrooms with different teachers would be quite varied.

What about time-varying covariates?

This is really an extension of the last problem, or maybe another way of saying the same thing. For studies that propose large-scale, nationally representative samples and longitudinal designs (all of the studies proposed in this section) there seems to me to be a systematic problem. One could envision exposure to educational technology (however it is measured) as itself varying over time. As I understand the analytic models proposed here, that would suggest that measures of educational technology exposure changed over time. The treatment in an analysis of covariance design itself varies over time. None of the authors actually addressed this, but one solution might be to treat such variables as time-varying covariates in a complex multilevel design. Under those circumstances, other classroom conditions might also vary over time (e.g., classroom composition or teachers' professional preparation). Even if it were possible to validly and reliably measure outcomes other than scores on standardized tests, in order to estimate their growth over time, the treatment itself (and other covariates) is changing also.

How do we analyze change in outcomes?

The Rumberger and Means et al. chapters mentioned using growth curve analysis with HLM. However, in the longitudinal studies these authors proposed, it seemed that the number of time points for assessing achievement or other outcomes was three or four and no more. Even with the assessment scores (e.g., standardized tests) that are amenable to equating, it is impossible to estimate students' individual growth trajectories and conduct growth curve analysis with only three or four time points. So the analysis would mostly estimate linear growth (either with change scores as outcomes, or in an analysis of covariance design). This is even more problematic with other kinds of outcomes—performance assessments, engagement, academic self-concept, or aspirations. Many of these authors argued, convincingly and appropriately, for the use of assessments that were more complex and sensitive than standardized test scores to measure the impact of technology use. But using such measures to evaluate change is problematic given that assessment experts remain concerned about the reliability and validity of such measures.

FINAL WORDS

It has been a pleasure for me to read such ambitious evaluation designs, especially because there seems to be a trend in the research and education communities against evaluations with such complex designs. The authors of the chapters discussed in Part III have substantial expertise in designs to evaluate educational innovations and interventions in general, and others are very familiar with educational technology in particular. I have raised, in my concluding comments, some issues that creep in only when designs are this ambitious. Hopefully, no one will see these issues as representing insurmountable problems for a large-scale evaluation of educational technology to move forward. With any ambitious plan, new problems arise. However, new problems also represent new challenges. With the rapid development of educational technology, new analytic methods have become available that make such evaluations stronger. But they also have data needs that make large sample sizes and complex designs more important. Hopefully, our nation's schools will soon take part in a large-scale evaluation of the impact of educational technology, and some of the people who have devised these ambitious plans will be at the forefront of such an effort.

Part IV

WHAT POLICYMAKERS AND ADMINISTRATORS CAN DO

A natural question someone reading this volume might ask is "Why don't we have the research we need on educational technology's effectiveness?" Earlier sections of this book have provided some implicit answers to this question, but here we tackle it head on.

The seeming simplicity of the question "Is educational technology effective?" is deceptive. It is difficult to provide a good research-based answer because the question is in reality extremely complex. There is a vast array of different technologies that can be and are used in schools. Moreover, even for a single selected technology (e.g., Internet search), there are many ways in which it can be used (e.g., a search engine can be used to look for a specific piece of information, to browse resources related to a topic of interest, or to inventory all relevant information sources on a topic in order to build a profile of the amount and types of information available). Differences in context can also result in what is ostensibly the same technology use being very different in practice (e.g., the difference between what fourth graders do and what advanced high school students do when using the same software tools to build spreadsheets and generate graphs). What's more, even if we limit our research questions to effects on student learning, there are all kinds of different things technology developers, teachers, and administrators hope and expect that students will learn from their technology-supported experiences. Expressed goals run the gamut from greater appreciation of diverse cultural perspectives to deep understanding of chemical equilibrium, to basic computation skills, to fluency in using technology. Finally, "simple" questions about the effectiveness of technology ignore the fact that a particular use of technology is likely to have positive effects on learning for some kinds of students under some circumstances but not for others. Thus any given piece of educational technology research, if well designed and implemented, is likely to contribute a piece of the puzzle, but none will answer the question for all kinds of technology, all learning goals, and all kinds of students and contexts.

A second reason why we are lacking a strong research base for making decisions about the application and implementation of educational technology is the low level of funding for such research. The Panel on Educational Technology of the President's Committee of Advisors on Science and Technology (PCAST) issued a report in 1997 noting the low level of investment in educational research in general and research on educational technology in particular. The panel argued that the investment in research in this area should be comparable in scope to that in pharmaceutical research—specifically calling for an annual investment of $1.5 billion. In 2003 the funding level for research on the learning impacts of technology-supported innovations (as described in the next section of this volume) is well under a tenth of that. The funding that does exist is mostly in the form of relatively small set-asides for evaluation, which are included as part of a technology development or implementation grant. While these evaluation components when aggregated across scores of grants do comprise millions of dollars, each individual evaluation is small in scope. The strong designs that research methodology experts advocate cannot be implemented in a myriad of small studies and with such small pockets of funding.

Finally, the research community itself must take some responsibility for the absence of a coherent research base. At times there appears to be more interest in waging the methodology wars than in gaining consensus and framing guidelines around which methodological approaches are most suited for which questions and circumstances. There has been little appetite for sharing instruments, linking studies, or systematically aggregating findings across studies as the authors in *Evaluating Educational Technology* have urged. During the emergence of learning technologies in the 1980s, we saw a flurry of research activity by Kulik and Kulik (1991), as well as by Shymansky, Kyle, and Alport (1983), to collect studies of similar technology applications and meta-analyze the effects of computer-based instruction when compared to conventional methods of teaching the same content. In the last 15 years, however, as learning technologies have proliferated and the targeted learning outcomes have become more diverse, educational researchers have conducted fewer syntheses that systematically accumulate findings across multiple studies. In part, the lack of research syntheses stems from the paucity of controlled studies with learning measures that are both appropriate for the intervention under study and of broad enough importance to be of interest to the public and other research groups.

Technology developers tend to assess students' learning within the confines of their software system. Those who do attempt to compare students using their technology to students learning by other means are inclined to use assessments that are specific to the content covered by their technology intervention. These assessments are generally developed for this specific purpose and have not been used widely either for educational or for research purposes. Leaving aside for the moment the serious issue of the technical quality of these assessments, it is difficult to know whether the material on these assessments is something students who did not experience the technology are taught and expected to know—that is, whether the material and skills are really critical, important learning or merely some intriguing concepts from the perspective of one particular research group. As long as researchers and educators are interested in assessing different learning outcomes, the world of practice and the world of research will remain estranged.

POLICYMAKERS AS RESEARCH FUNDERS AND PARTNERS

The discussion above suggests that there is substantial room for improvement in the way educational technology gets evaluated and in the way in which technology's impact on learning is studied. We believe that education policymakers can play a significant role in bringing higher standards and greater usability to this research enterprise. The crux of our argument is the importance of partnerships between policymakers and evaluators. We urge policymakers responsible for making decisions about educational programs to treat evaluation not as an arcane service provided by outsiders in order to meet requirements for accountability but rather as a tool to support their decision making.

Careful thought early on concerning the types of decisions that must be made about a program (e.g., whether to begin on a pilot basis or mandate implementation across a system; the amount and type of teacher professional development to be provided in connection with the intervention) will help policymakers articulate their research and evaluation needs. In this volume, as in *Evaluating Educational Technology*, we suggest that different methodological approaches are best suited to different kinds of questions. The choice of a research approach should be driven by the central question motivating the study rather than by a sense of orthodoxy with respect to particular methodologies. We believe that the policymakers and administrators responsible for making educational decisions should assert their right to frame the questions that will guide the evaluation of the programs for which they are responsible.

In our experience, many educational policymakers are unaccustomed to this role. We suggest that policymakers begin planning an implementation for a new education initiative by interacting with evaluators who can help them think through the theory underlying the intervention. To explicate this theory, policymakers must first of all gain clarity about the nature of the outcomes that the intervention is expected to enhance. Do policymakers care about scores on the SAT-9, a thorough understanding of fractions, getting all students prepared for algebra by grade 8, or instilling a love of mathematics? Is the main goal to raise average performance, to increase the proportion of students functioning at a level deemed acceptable, or to reduce the gap between performance by different ethnic groups, language backgrounds, or genders? If the policymakers' answer to these questions is "all of the above," evaluators need to push them to clarify relative priorities, since there will never be the research resources to measure all outcomes of potential value and interest.

Evaluators can also work as facilitators in meetings of multiple policymakers and stakeholders who may hold different views concerning an intervention's most important goals. Differences of opinion may make people uncomfortable, but it is better to air these differences at an early stage in the evaluative process rather than after an expensive study has been conducted.

Once the most important desired outcomes are clarified, policymakers can work with their evaluators to specify the mechanisms through which the intervention is expected to bring about these outcomes. This means going far beyond naming the intervention to describe its key components and how they will be implemented. Sending *Reader Rabbit* to the district warehouse will not be enough to improve student reading, but what will? Which teachers in what grade levels will use the software for which of their students? How much time do students need with the software, and what do teachers need to do to support this activity? If essential aspects of the intervention are articulated in this manner, evaluators can measure them and avoid wasting money on measuring outcomes in places where the intervention has not really gone into effect.

Many technology-based interventions are complex and make heavy demands on the system for infrastructure support (e.g., convenient access to Internet resources in all classrooms). For this reason, a significant investment in what evaluators call formative research, to help understand implementation processes and how the intervention can be improved, is prudent before embarking on a summative study of an intervention's effectiveness.

Setting forth an intervention's critical implementation steps and their assumed time frame can also help both the evaluator and the policymaker sponsoring the evaluation gain insight into when it would be reasonable to expect the desired outcomes to be in evidence. To take an obvious example, if one wants to know whether a program that teaches systems administration skills to high school sophomores really helps them get better jobs after graduation, there is no way around the need to let several years lapse for the students to complete high school, and perhaps community college or a university degree as well. If the program's outcomes are evaluated too quickly, it becomes impossible to tell if a lack of positive outcomes is attributable to inadequate implementation of the program components or to an ineffective program that may not be suitable for use in the local context. More subtle forms of premature evaluation occur in cases where an intervention requires teachers to obtain proficiency in technology use or pedagogical methods that require multiple years of practice to acquire proficiency. If there is insufficient time allowed for teachers to develop an appropriate level of proficiency with the technology or methods, it will be difficult to discern whether a lack of program outcomes should be attributed to poor mastery of the necessary skills by teachers or to an ineffective program.

Policymakers also need to specify any particular settings, teacher groups, students, or circumstances that are of particular policy interest. A *convenience sample*—collecting data from those students and teachers who are readily available—will provide findings that may not generalize to schools and students in general; policymakers can feel more confident making decisions based on evaluations with samples of schools or students that truly represent their district (or state). If it is important to know whether the intervention is effective in urban elementary schools or in classrooms where over a third of the students are classified as English language learners, enough of these settings must be included in the evaluation to enable reliable estimates of outcomes in these circumstances.

Policymakers also can educate their evaluators concerning constraints within the system that are likely to affect the intervention and research options (for example, state testing dates and time spent focusing on test preparation). Policymakers have extensive knowledge of the factors influencing practice in their jurisdictions, and that knowledge should inform evaluation design and implementation.

Few education policymakers are researchers by training and they do not need to try to become researchers. They should seek specialized expertise to guide them through issues of evaluation design and data analysis. What we are urging, however, is that policymakers bring the expertise they have—their knowledge of the education system, their deep understandings of the local context, their networks with other professionals who can support the evaluation, and their goals for improvement—to a joint endeavor of studying, documenting, and understanding the effects of educational technology. We recognize the severe demands placed on policymakers' time, but argue that the more time and effort they put into the framing of evaluations of their programs, the more the local or state education agencies that they serve will benefit.

POLICYMAKERS AND ADMINISTRATORS AS RESEARCH CONSUMERS

Thus far we have discussed what policymakers can do to increase the likelihood that evaluations they sponsor will in fact serve their needs. Here we discuss what education policymakers can do to become intelligent users of research and evaluation studies that have been conducted in the past. With the passage of No Child Left Behind, which includes (in Title II, Part D), encouragement for the implementation of technology-supported, research-based instructional methods, policymakers are explicitly called upon to be able to justify selected innovations on the basis of research.

Descriptions of research in general, and certainly those of technology-supported educational innovations, tend to gloss over important characteristics of the intervention, the students who received the treatment, the context, and the outcomes. Headlines such as "Technology Increases Student Skills" or "Technology Fails to Help Students Learn" don't tell the reader what the intervention was (e.g., on-line phonics instruction or Internet search engines), where and how it was implemented (e.g., in one particular middle school or statewide for fourth graders; for two hours a day for nine months or 30 minutes a week for a semester), or what kinds of learning were measured (e.g., reading comprehension, ability to recognize correctly spelled words, composite test scores). The evidence provided by research and evaluation studies is generally much more constrained. The savvy research consumer examines multiple studies, keeping track of their specific interventions, contexts, and outcomes, and hones in on those that address the research questions, outcomes, populations, and settings of particular concern.

Policymakers may want to seek trusted advisors with research expertise to help them review and summarize the research base. They should beware of publications that blur the distinction between advocacy and research summary. Educational technology has been an area in which advocacy (both for and against technology) has often worn the cloak of research summary. Any time a large number of education studies are presented and all point to the same conclusion (either favorable or unfavorable), the research consumer should question the level of objectivity in selecting studies to review and summarizing their findings.

Robert Murphy and his colleagues have developed a guide for educational policymakers and practitioners trying to make sense of claims concerning the effectiveness of educational software (Murphy, Yarnell, Penuel, & Huang, 2003). Available on-line, the guide is intended to help inform decisions concerning the purchase of software for the purpose of raising achievement test scores. The authors walk the user through the process of evaluating the research backing for a piece of educational software in terms of (1) its applicability to the decision maker's classroom, school, or district; (2) the quality of the research design with respect to the nature of the claims made; and (3) an examination of the way in which student achievement was measured. Frequently encountered weaknesses in studies of the effectiveness of specific pieces of software are described in a section on "red flags." A "buyer's worksheet" can be downloaded and filled out as a way to summarize the applicability and quality of the research support for a piece of software. Murphy et al. (2003) conclude the guide with a caveat for those making decisions concerning software purchases:

> You should never base any decision about the effectiveness of educational technology on the results of just one study. You should make your decision only after collecting multiple pieces of evidence, including other studies that document the effectiveness of the program for schools and students like your own. (http://www.ncrel.org/tech/claims)

At some point, policymakers interested in gaining insights into research on the impacts of educational technologies may find assistance in the What Works Clearinghouse. The federal government has funded the development of the What Works Clearinghouse (U.S. Department of Education, Institute of Educational Sciences, 2002), an effort to pull together effectiveness research on selected education topics, rate the quality of the available research evidence, and present it in a form that policymakers and practitioners can use.

The What Works Clearinghouse (WWC) should not be construed as the educational equivalent of the Good Housekeeping Seal of Approval, however. Given the complexity of both the education and the research enterprises, the WWC cannot simply provide a list of approved instructional methods or technologies. A policymaker will always need to examine the research base in light of the particular settings and students for which the intervention is being considered and in light of the outcomes of interest.

The What Works Clearinghouse is beginning with the development of criteria for judging the quality of research studies that have the measurement of causal relationships between interventions and outcomes as their primary purpose. The WWC team concluded that research quality is multidimensional, requiring separate ratings on dimensions such as the definition of the intervention and outcomes, the evidence for causality, and the relevance of the participants and environments involved in the study. Educational technology is not among the first set of topic areas, but one or another technology use could well become the subject of later reviews, and interested individuals have the opportunity to nominate topics for review at the WWC Web site (http://www.W-W-C.org/topicnom.html).

Even when the WWC reviews educational technology topics, it will not answer all policymakers' needs. As noted earlier in this part and in *Evaluating Educational Technology,* the main questions that must be answered are not always those of causal connections between interventions and average impacts. Many times there is an interest in issues of implementation, in gaining insights into the prerequisites for greater frequency of use of certain technology tools or technology-supported pedagogies.

HOW POLICYMAKERS AND EVALUATORS CAN COLLABORATE

We believe the most useful evaluations are those in which policymakers collaborate with evaluators in the design, instrumentation, interpretation, and reporting of the evaluation study. Such collaboration ensures that the evaluation will be aligned with local needs and will be credible among stakeholders. The evaluation design process begins with the policymaker posing questions that may or may not require that a new evaluation be conducted. Some policymakers' questions can be answered through reviews of databases and quantitative and qualitative summaries of prior evaluation results, while other questions require that an evaluator be consulted and a new evaluation be designed. In each case, the policymaker needs to locate appropriate resources that can serve as starting points for the actions to follow.

Policymakers may choose to engage researchers to help identify and synthesize the relevant literature on topics of interest. If prior summaries of research results are insufficient to address the questions posed, then the policymaker may consult an evaluator for the needed expertise. If a new evaluation is to be designed, we would encourage the policymaker and evaluator to collaborate in activities that are fundamental to the design of an evaluation that is sensitive to the needs of the local setting and that collects the kinds of evidence needed to answer the questions of concern to deci-

Figure 4.1. Policymaker and Evaluator Collaboration

Collaborative Consultation with Evaluator to . . .

Clarify Evaluation Questions

- Clarify goals of the evaluation
- Formulate potential evaluation questions of interest to stakeholders and audiences
- Facilitate meetings of stakeholders when diverse points of view exist
- Determine available resources (time and dollars)
- Prioritize evaluation goals and questions
- Specify what decisions will need to be made

Describe Technology-Supported Intervention

- Describe the technology-supported intervention
- Specify the theory of how the intervention will have its intended effects
- Specify the mechanisms that have been used to implement the intervention

Specify Context and Degree of Implementation

- Identify the school/district/state/federal policy context
- Identify teacher and school district personnel who will participate in the evaluation
- Identify student populations who are served by the intervention and who will participate in its evaluation
- Specify the technology infrastructure currently in place
- Specify the general level or degree of implementation of the intervention that has taken place

Review Student Outcomes

- Determine the purpose of the assessment (e.g., learning of facts, principles, problem solving, inquiry, technology proficiency, change in attitudes)
- Determine how test administration takes place (e.g., standardized, on-line, collaborative, or individual)
- Determine the kinds of item formats needed (e.g., multiple choice, open-ended, performance assessments)
- Determine the scoring and analysis needed (e.g., number and percent correct, percentiles, competency-based categorical ratings)

Select Evaluation/Design

- Consider alternative evaluation designs (e.g., case studies, experiment, quasi-experiment)
- Consider sources of data needed (e.g., teachers, students, parents)
- Consider data collection technique (e.g., survey, observation, interview, performance assessment)

Stipulate Reporting

- Agree upon types of data to be reported
- Set out a schedule for reporting
- Discuss audiences for evaluation reports
- Discuss alternative reporting formats and technical level at which reports will be aimed

83

sion makers. Figure 4.1 provides more detail about the set of activities on which policymakers and evaluators can collaborate to produce an evaluation that is both rigorous and useful. Each is described below.

Clarify Evaluation Questions

As the first step illustrates, policymakers are advised to engage with stakeholders in clarifying the evaluation's purposes, goals, and questions. Of particular importance is the effort to specify what decisions will need to be made based on the evaluation results. For example, will the data be used to refine the way a particular technology-supported intervention is being used, to implement a particular intervention more fully, or to make a decision to continue or terminate the use of the intervention? During this initial activity, the policymaker and evaluator should clarify whether the evaluation will be formative or summative.

Describe Technology-Supported Intervention

The policymaker (or more commonly a group of policymakers and key stakeholders) should work with the evaluator to explicate and document a full description of the particular technology-supported intervention to be evaluated. One way this description may be represented is as a *theory of change* (alternatively called a *theory of action*) that identifies the links between implementation of program components and the short- and long-term outcomes that are the intervention's goals. The evaluator can help elicit the intervention theory from policymakers and stakeholders through interviews or through facilitating meetings designed to get at program assumptions and to bring to light any missing steps in implementation plans, unrealistic assumptions, or competing views regarding goals and mechanisms. Specifying the details of the intervention, especially the conditions needed for successful implementation, is essential. Without knowing what constitutes a fully implemented intervention, it is impossible to separate an ineffective intervention from one that is poorly implemented.

Specify Context and Degree of Implementation

The policymaker and the evaluator should work together also to specify the context in which the evaluation will take place. The policymaker's role is to provide a rich and accurate portrait of the local settings in which the evaluation will unfold. This would include features of the school, district, or state educational system such as policy mandates, demographic characteristics of students and teachers, educational reform history, technology infrastructure, and the nature and amount of teacher professional development experiences. In addition, desired performances or student learning outcomes need to be described and the conditions that support these performances are best specified by practitioners and policymakers who are deeply familiar with the local context.

A key element of this process is estimating the degree to which the technology-supported intervention has been implemented. The policymaker and evaluator can ask questions such as, "Are all the sites where this intervention was implemented active? If not, why? If they are active, to what degree have they implemented the key components of the intervention? Have they implemented the intervention with the target groups? Have teachers at the various sites had access to the technology and the professional development needed to attain proficiency in the use of the intervention with their students? Were sites expected to faithfully implement the intervention? Or was local adaptation expected? Do the implementation sites vary in the ways they have institutionalized the intervention?" It is useful for the policymaker and evaluator to discuss these issues of implementation in detail. While typically they will not have systematically collected data available to answer all these questions, the questions need to be addressed in order to understand whether (1) the intervention has been implemented sufficiently to conduct a full-fledged summative evaluation of the intervention's effects or (2) there have been significant lapses in the implementation of the intervention that require evaluation of the implementation process itself. Going through this assessment of implementation conditions can confirm or disconfirm the original purposes planned for the proposed evaluation.

Review Student Outcomes

An important component of collaborative evaluation design involves identification of the student outcomes to be assessed. The student outcomes that are the goals of the interventions will have been discussed as part of developing the intervention theory of change. At this stage, the evaluator and policymaker move toward agreement on how to measure the desired outcomes. There may be multiple outcomes of interest in the proposed evaluation, ranging from higher level thinking processes and problem solving, to competencies in particular subject area domains, to proficiency using particular technologies, to changes in behaviors, such as school attendance and application to postsecondary education. In this review, the policymaker, with input from local practitioners, can provide advice on how the key outcomes should be measured (e.g., through capture of data elements in district databases, portfolios, administration of paper-and-pencil short-answer tests, essays, on-line performance assessments) and the way these outcomes will be reported. Ideally, the evaluator's technical expertise in instrumentation and assessment development will be coupled with the policymaker's knowledge of the local context, stakeholder preferences, and available resources. The value of this collaboration will be reflected in the use of sound assessment practices supported by consensus in the local setting that the outcome measures and the formats used are credible indicators of valued results for students.

Select Evaluation Design

The collaborative activities described above provide the basis for constructing an evaluation design and specifying the information-gathering techniques that will be used to collect data. The choice of design, while requiring evaluation expertise, also requires buy-in among policymakers. Regardless of whether the design is a random-assignment experiment, a series of case studies, or a longitudinal survey, the evaluation is unlikely to succeed without policymaker support. Without leadership on the part of policymakers, the participant enthusiasm, logistics, and resources required to conduct the evaluation are unlikely to occur.

This is also the point in time when issues of student and parental permission, confidentiality, agreements with teacher unions, classroom observations, access to scarce resources, and other legal, logistical, and ethical aspects of the evaluative activity are likely to be considered. Policymaker engagement is fundamental in the planning of the evaluation, especially when parents, community members, and teachers are going to be asked to participate in the research.

Stipulate Reporting Formats and Schedule

The usability of evaluation findings depends not only upon sound designs and faithful study implementation but also upon the way in which evaluation findings are communicated to those whose practice and decisions can benefit from the research. Advance discussion concerning the audiences, purposes, timing, level of detail, and format of study approaches can enhance the usefulness of the evaluation.

CONCLUSION

Ellen Lagemann (2002) has coined the phrase *useable knowledge in education* to refer to professional knowledge that can be used in practice.

Lagemann describes *disciplinary research* as the effort to develop a knowledge base by defining important concepts or variables and uncovering relationships among them that can be formulated as lawlike statements ("greater time on task leads to greater learning") that will apply across contexts and instances, "other things being equal." Lagemann argues that educators need to take the knowledge developed through disciplinary research and combine it with understandings concerning the factors that might affect an intervention and obtained outcomes in the particular setting where they are working. In a similar vein, our call for a more interactive partnership between evaluators and educational policymakers is intended to promote (1) research and evaluation that address the questions and decisions that policymakers and practitioners care about and (2) the use of research to inform what educators do. Contextualized research can help enhance educators' understanding of how a particular technology-supported intervention works with the students, teachers, and constraints that characterize the local education setting. This knowledge of how interventions play out in specific contexts can be combined with what Lagemann calls disciplinary research to provide knowledge that policymakers and practitioners can use.

A Blueprint for a National Research Agenda to Evaluate Educational Technology

Barbara Means
Geneva D. Haertel

While this volume advocates the initiation of a major, coordinated federal investment in research on the effects of educational technology, it is important to recognize that the federal government already supports a number of relevant research programs. Here we describe current and recent federal support for educational technology research and then proceed to describe the kinds of research programs that would be needed to implement the recommendations of the authors who contributed to *Evaluating Educational Technology*.

EXISTING FEDERAL SUPPORT FOR LEARNING TECHNOLOGY RESEARCH

U.S. Department of Education Support for Technology Research

The Department of Education has funded a variety of research efforts to inform educators, policymakers, and the public about the effects of learning technology. Most of this funding has come in the form of support for evaluation activities conducted as part of implementation programs involving technology. Thus these efforts are what Becker and Lovitts (in the research volume) call "project-linked" studies on early-stage innovations. The Technology Innovation Challenge Grants (TICG), for example, funded local education agencies to partner with universities, businesses, and research organizations to develop and demonstrate new ways to creatively use technology for learning. Starting in 1995, the Department of Education awarded 96 Challenge Grant projects at a combined level of over $500 million. Although the funding primarily supported technology design and implementation activities, grantees were required to spend 10% of their funds on evaluation activities, thus generating something in the neighborhood of $50 million for TICG-related evaluation studies over a period of 6 years. Similarly, Star Schools distance learning project grantees and teacher preparation programs receiving grants for Preparing Tomorrow's Teachers to Use Technology (PTTT) were required to include evaluation as one of their project components.

Another impetus for evaluations of technology has been federal educational technology funding block grants to states. This began under the Clinton administration with the Technology Literacy Challenge Fund giving money to every state to help schools integrate technology by supporting improved applications of technology and teacher training and preparation. States and local education entities could use the funds for technology support in a variety of ways, including support for computers, connectivity, professional development, and technical support. Under the Bush administration, Title II of the NCLB Act expands the potential uses schools can make of federal technology funds flowing through their states. In exchange for this flexibility, the authorizing legislation calls on states to develop performance measurement systems to determine the effectiveness of educational technology programs funded under this act, including the demonstration of how funded technology integration is enabling students to meet challenging state academic content and achievement standards.

Project evaluations performed in conjunction with technology implementation grants are an important source of information for an individual project seeking to refine its design and in a few instances have brought national attention to projects that appear to be particularly effective. It has, however, proved difficult to integrate evaluation findings across previous projects funded by the Department of Education to provide evidence of empirically derived "lessons learned" with respect to the effects of technology on student learning. The various projects have had different goals, used different outcome measures, and in many cases did not incorporate strong evaluation designs.

Another way in which research on the effects of learning technology could be funded is through direct grants from the U.S. Department of Education. Relatively little funding of research on technology has come through the department's field-initiated research program, however. A review of 1999 grantees, for example, found that only one of 20 funded field-initiated projects involved the use of technology in the approach under investigation.

A third way in which the U.S. Department of Education has funded studies on educational technology is through contract research. Research coming out of the National Center for Education Statistics has been primarily a matter of collecting statistics on technology access (e.g., the proportion of classrooms in different types of schools with Internet access). The former Planning and Evaluation Studies Office within the U.S. Department of Education did let several contracts in the educational technology area. These Integrated Studies of Educational Technology (ISET) used a common set of surveys of districts, schools, and classrooms to examine current practice with respect to educational technology. One of these studies, for example, looked at what schools and districts have done with E-rate funding (Puma, Chaplin, & Pape, 2000). Another study sought evidence concerning the effects of support from the Technology Literacy Challenge Fund on teachers' learning to integrate technology into instruction (Adelman et al., 2002). The survey findings from the ISET studies provided a broad picture of current practices with respect to educational technology use and supports for teachers' learning about technology, but did not address questions about the effects of technology on student learning. More recently, the National Educational Technology Trends Study (NETTS) is examining how states are using technology funding provided through Title II of No Child Left Behind.

National Science Foundation Research Support for Technology Research

The Education and Human Resources Directorate within the National Science Foundation (NSF) has a track record of several decades of funding for the development of new curricular and instructional approaches supported by technology in the areas of mathematics and science education. Most recently, this tradition is carried on through NSF's Research on Learning and Education (ROLE) program, which issued its first call for proposals in November 1999. ROLE's stated aim is to enable the integration of research on learning into broader educational and social contexts.

The ROLE research program is organized around the context and grain size for the research (e.g., brain research, fundamental learning research, research in formal and informal educational settings, learning in complex educational systems) and does not include a separate category or priority for technology-related research. However, the solicitation does cite technology as a crosscutting theme. Technology-related proposals are encouraged: "In order to improve quality, accessibility and efficiency of SMET [science, mathematics, engineering and technology] education, ROLE promotes the use of new and evolving information technologies" (ROLE, 1999, p.6). To the extent that ROLE projects incorporate research on the effects of learning technology on student learning, this research is project-linked. While helpful in informing the research and development efforts, these projects are unlikely to provide evidence of a type or scale that policymakers demand. In these grants, the research on technology effectiveness is just one component, and often a fairly small part, of the entire project. The ROLE solicitation explicitly discourages proposals whose primary emphasis is evaluating the effectiveness of a given innovation: "ROLE is not an evaluation program; rather, it discourages submissions of proposals whose primary purpose is to conduct evaluations of other projects, including activities that [NSF's] EHR [Education and Human Resources] Divisions support" (p. 10). With an FY2000 annual budget of $8 million, ROLE supports research on new educational approaches supported by technology but is not designed to address questions concerning the effectiveness of educational technology more generally.

Interagency Education Research Initiative (IERI) Support for Technology Research

In 1999 the U.S. Department of Education, National Science Foundation, and National Institute of Child Health and Human Development initiated a joint research program focusing on reading, mathematics, and science, with an emphasis on projects that integrate technology. The Interagency Education Research Initiative (IERI) program announcement is explicit in calling for "scaling up" research on interventions with preliminary evidence of effectiveness. The purpose of IERI grants is to "identify conditions under which effective evidence-based interventions to improve K–12 student learning and achievement succeed when applied on a large scale" (IERI, 2002, p.2). Thus this research program seeks to fund research on the effectiveness of "mature" innovations. The program solicitation explicitly encourages experimental designs involving random assignment. The IERI program is quite consistent with the themes stressed by the methodology experts in this volume, including systematic investigation of implementation and context variables. Compared to the PCAST report's call for $1.5 billion annually in research on teaching and learning with technology, however, the IERI funding levels are modest indeed. Some $30 million was awarded under this program in 1999; $38 million in 2000; and $60 million in 2001.

CONSIDERATIONS FOR ORGANIZATIONAL STRUCTURE

We presume that a major research program on the effective use of technology in education would require a federal investment, raising the issue of the organizational home for such a program. As described above, existing funding for such research comes from a variety of agencies and does not reflect any overarching comprehensive framework. Our assumption is that locating the effort within a lead agency would increase the likelihood of integration and coherence.

Technology can potentially support any educational function, content area, or grade level. Thus technology is what Scriven (1991) has called a *transdiscipline*. We could easily take the foci for the various research programs within the U.S. Department of Education and create a research program entitled "Technology and..." for each of them (e.g., Technology and Student Achievement, Curriculum, and Assessment; Technology and Postsecondary Education, Libraries, and Lifelong Learning). And in fact, when the institutes within the Office of Educational Research and Improvement (now superseded by the Institute of Education Sciences) were set up, technology was considered a crosscutting theme. Ideally, the study of technology supports would be integrated with research on critical questions in every area of teaching and learning. Often, however, this has not happened in practice. Technology has received relatively little emphasis in many subject area content standards, discussions of teacher preparation, and education reform initiatives outside those explicitly labeled as *technology initiatives*. Our review of the Department of Education's *Catalog of School Reform Programs*, for example, found that technology was a significant feature in less than a third of the 33 whole-school reform models. Technology receives even less consideration as a force for school improvement in the widely influential document *Turning Around Low-Performing Schools: A Guide for State and Local Leaders* (Doherty & Abernathy, 1998). All of this suggests that the question of the organizational home for research on teaching and learning with technology is not a trivial one.

The potential pitfall in setting up a separate technology research program (or for that matter, a separate technology curriculum or assessment) is the risk that technology will become a separate track, poorly integrated with core educational endeavors. Those with strong technology backgrounds are likely to be attracted to the research program, but there is danger of begetting an engineering emphasis, rather than interplay between technology and core teaching and learning issues. On the other hand, when educational technology research is made a part of a research program defined on the basis of a subject area (e.g., early reading or history) or target population (English language learners), opportunities for integration increase, but technology may get token treatment or be ignored completely. Researchers interested in technology's contribution to the area may be discouraged from working with the program or may find it difficult to win support for their ideas. Peer review panels set up by such programs often lack individuals with a technology background, meaning that panelists are either uninterested in technology or unaware of what has already been done. In the latter case, panelists have a hard time distinguishing technology-based proposals that are both feasible and potentially groundbreaking from those that are technically unrealistic or mere rehashes of relatively common practice.

Some hybrid model, with a specifically designated program of research on learning technologies but also with requirements for coordination with the overall educational research and reform agendas, appears the most promising strategy overall. In our recommendations below, we envision such a program with some of its components integrated with existing educational research units and some existing as identifiable technology and education initiatives with their own visibility and support. Care would have to be taken to make sure that the technology research agenda is well coordinated with what we have called the "mainstream" research in each of the areas targeted for federal investments in education research.

CONSIDERATIONS FOR DEGREE OF DIRECTION

Another issue that needs to be considered in planning a major program of research is the extent to which the focus and methods of that research arise out of federal planning efforts versus coming from the field. Policymakers have to make trade-offs between the desire to have certain kinds of research done and the desire to be open to good ideas arising from the individual investigators in the research community. Some of the current federally funded research on educational technology is performed under contract, with the government stipulating the nature and scale of the data it wants collected. In the past, most of this work has been the collection of survey data on technology access and frequency of use, or compilations of previously collected information. Other federal research programs have employed the opposite strategy, supporting field-initiated research, that is, those research proposals coming from outside the government that receive the highest ratings from panels of reviewers. In the Department of Education, most field-initiated research programs have not entertained proposals of a size commensurate with the research strategies recommended by our chapter authors.

A major program of research on learning technology including all of the components we describe below would probably employ a wide range of contractual arrangements. A vehicle often used by the Department of Education that has not been used in the field of research on learning technology effects is the funding of a national lab or center with this mission. (Centers focused on educational technology *implementation* have been funded.) Center proposals respond to federal agency statements of need for research in a priority area, but leave the proposing organizations substantial room for setting the particulars of their own research programs.

In the case of research on the effects of technology-supported educational innovations, the Department of Education may want to look to practices of the National Institutes for Health (NIH). The NIH uses two primary strategies for harnessing the ideas and energies of multiple research organizations to an overarching research program with common measures and shared data sets. Under cooperative agreements, the NIH sets up an *intermediary organization* within one of its own institutes. NIH researchers stipulate measures and data collection protocols and maintain a central data repository at NIH. This approach requires the availability of a set of practicing research scientists within the government agency. Alternatively, for major health studies (in the $50 million range), an NIH institute typically releases a separate announcement for a coordinating center (housed outside the government) that will serve this function for multiple research and data collection organizations, also working under contract. The coordinating centers typically have the research qualifications to be a data collection center themselves (and sometimes the same organization will win both types of contract). The coordinating center develops instruments, writes data collection protocols, serves as a data repository, conducts core data analyses, and makes the data available to the other investigators. The coordinating center supports the latter activity by making sure that analysts using the data set define variables in the same way, so that seemingly contradictory results are not caused by differences in variable labeling or definition.

PROPOSED FOUR-PART TECHNOLOGY RESEARCH AGENDA

In the remainder of this chapter, we will make a case for a four-part federal educational technology research agenda, designed to address the larger research questions that have not been answered by prior individual project-linked research or evaluation studies. We propose four distinctive but interrelated research and development missions:

- Research on technology use in schools
- Evaluative research on teaching and learning with technology

- Information system for educational context and implementation measures
- Initiative for twenty-first-century skills, indicators, and assessments

Research on Technology Use in Schools

This research program would examine the frequencies and correlates of common and emerging *naturally occurring practices.* These are practices that are being widely implemented in U.S. schools without special funding from sources external to the education system (i.e., atypical levels of support from research or commercial organizations developing the technology). Research under this program would attempt to answer questions about how technology is being used in different kinds of schools (e.g., those serving different populations or those with different curriculum and instructional philosophies) and in different subject areas and grade levels, and would relate these uses to observed outcomes. The TLC survey conducted by Hank Becker and his colleagues (1999), which examined the relationship between teacher beliefs about pedagogy and teacher's use of technology with their students, is an example of the type of research such a program might sponsor. This component of the research agenda could also include major longitudinal studies of technology use in schools (as proposed by Rumberger, 2003, and Means, Wagner, Haertel, & Javitz, 2003), possibly in connection with an existing national longitudinal study. Detailed case studies describing the implementation of technology innovations and the influences of various factors within the classroom, school, and district contexts would also fall into this line of descriptive research on "what is."

More specific topics that might become areas of research within this program include the following:

- Internet research
- Use of basic skills educational software with Title I students
- Technology use for English language learners
- Computer-based writing instruction

An important component of this research would be empirical tests of the effects of providing different forms of training and support for teachers' integration of technology with instruction. Both preservice and inservice education and support, and both technology-based and off-line forms of teacher learning, need to be investigated.

This research should be conducted with an eye toward informing policy discussions around state and district accountability systems that are providing rewards and sanctions related to the integration of technology and teachers' demonstrated technology proficiency. An important research question given different state strategies for increasing teachers' ability to use technology within classrooms (e.g., requiring a technology course as part of teacher preparation as opposed to requiring teachers to pass a technology proficiency test in order to obtain a credential) is the effect of any such system on the teaching and learning that occurs within those teachers' classrooms. This same research program could encourage integration of graduate schools of education and local K–12 school systems through professional development programs that integrate research into practice with teacher learning.

Evaluative Research on Teaching and Learning with Technology

In addition to understanding "what is," policymakers need to gain an understanding of "what could be." Specifically, they would like to know how to maximize the benefits of technology use in schools for student learning. This goal needs to be addressed through a quite different line of research, one that examines student learning effects of well-defined projects or innovations involving technology.

Given the size, breadth, and complexity of the research agenda, we propose setting up a responsible organization, a research center sponsoring and overseeing multiple studies on the effectiveness of technology in addressing topics established as priorities for federal education research generally (e.g., early reading and middle school mathematics).

In addition to contextualized evaluations illustrating the interplay between research and practice described as Pasteur's Quadrant (Stokes, 1997), the Research Center on Teaching and Learning with Technology we envision would support random-assignment and quasi experiments to investigate the effects of mature innovations. Because it is important to be looking to the future and to provide a research base that can influence both commercial and noncommercial technology innovators as well, this center would also sponsor proof-of-concept studies exploring the value of new technologies (e.g., wireless Internet devices and services).

Thus we imagine this research center sponsoring research employing a range of methodologies. Quality criteria and conditions of applicability for each methodology should be elucidated, as a guide both to individuals responding to program solicitations and to the proposal review process. Wherever appropriate, the research sponsored by this center would incorporate the common context measures and the assessments developed as part of the final two components of the research agenda (described below). Aggregation of findings across studies could be further supported through clustering studies of innovations with similar learning goals and the efforts of a nongovernmental intermediary organization, as suggested above. This work could also be supported by a network of *sentinel schools* or test beds, as suggested by several of the authors in *Evaluating Educational Technology*. A Research Center on Teaching and Learning with Technology would be appropriate as the sponsoring agency for this network. The schools participating in the network would become a test bed for coordinated studies of new technology approaches and innovations.

Information System for Educational Implementation and Context Measures

Many of the authors in *Evaluating Educational Technology* call for carefully documenting the context and the implementation effort within which technology-supported teaching and learning occur. These authors also advocate for researchers using the same measures in sets of coordinated, linked, or embedded studies. Examples of important contextual variables include teacher characteristics, teacher pedagogical beliefs and practices, professional development supports, school leadership, family use of technology, community engagement, technology infrastructure, presence of other educational reform programs, and the state and district accountability system in place. (In some cases, for example, for teacher professional development and technology infrastructure, documenting the status of a site with respect to the variable is tantamount to documenting a key aspect of implementation because the innovation's theory of change involves establishing a conducive context for the innovation.)

Among the implementation variables of interest would be whether the implementing agents understand the practice they are implementing and whether the beliefs and attitudes are consonant with that practice (Spillane, Reiser, & Reimer, 2002). Other aspects of implementation that could be documented might include the creation of formal and informal networks of teachers (Coburn, 2001) and the establishment of internal systems for measuring implementation progress. The chapter by Lesgold (2003) suggests how maturity models could be created for several variables that influence the implementation of innovations, such as people and instruction.

The importance of these factors in influencing educational outcomes is not limited to interventions involving technology, of course. The compilation of a set of standard definitions and instruments for measuring contextual and implementation variables would be a major support for educational research generally. To gain acceptance, the core set of contextual and implementation variables and associated definitions and instruments would have to be developed through an iterative consensus process. Educational research associations, education leadership and policy organizations, and agencies sponsoring teaching and learning research (not just research involving technology) should all be involved. To get the broadest possible benefit, this work should be carried out from an organizational home that spans the gamut of educational research (perhaps the National Center for Education Statistics). Definitions, rubrics, and instruments could be made available through the World Wide Web. (The Online Evaluation Resource Library [OERL] site at http://oerl.sri.com provides an example of the kind of easy-to-navigate interface that would be needed.)

Initiative for Twenty-First-Century Skills, Indicators, and Assessments

As many of the research chapter authors noted, many studies of the effects of technology-supported innovations are hindered by a lack of measures of student learning commensurate with the initiatives' goals. The kinds of mathematical reasoning and ability to predict the results of changes in rate that are among the key objectives for *SimCalc* (Kaput & Roschelle, 1998), for example, get little or no coverage in widely available standardized tests.

High-stakes testing programs that emphasize basic skills and factual knowledge concerning a broad range of topics (as opposed to deeper conceptual knowledge in a narrower range of fields) serve as disincentives for the use of innovative technology-supported programs that stress deep understanding of a few topics, and advanced problem solving and communication skills.

The principled design, development, and field testing of assessment instruments that are valid, reliable, and sensitive to instruction is a complex, time-consuming effort, and one that is not easily mastered by organizations with little experience in this area. As Baker and Herman (2003) pointed out, it is unrealistic to expect individual technology projects that support types of learning not well represented in off-the-shelf tests to develop their own measures in a context of limited funding. Moreover, neither private companies nor individual states are likely to amass the resources and expertise necessary to design, develop, field-test, and disseminate such assessments for all the grade levels and skill and knowledge areas we hope to address with technology. For this reason, we see the development of high-quality assessments of the kinds of skills called for by standards-setting bodies as appropriate for federal research and development support.

While the number of different content areas in which we might want to have better student assessments is virtually unlimited, there is a great deal of agreement around the need for assessments of certain generalizable information-seeking, analysis, and communication skills. These skills would provide a good focus for the first stage of this assessment development initiative. These are skills that employers say they need in twenty-first-century workers and that are stressed by standards-setting organizations both in content areas and in the area of technology itself.

There is considerable overlap across different standards-setting bodies in terms of the kinds of skills they believe students will need in an information society. These standards-setting bodies include the National Council of Teachers of Mathematics (NCTM), National Research Council (NRC), International Society for Technology in Education (ISTE), and the American Association for the Advancement of Science (AAAS). The fact that groups in science, mathematics, language arts, technology, and social studies all stress similar skills means that an assessment development effort built around these skills would have wide applicability.

Both the Secretary's Commission on Achieving Necessary Skills and the New Standards Project (Simmons & Resnick, 1993) have done useful work that provides a foundation for further efforts to provide high-quality assessments in these areas. Moreover, prospects for improved and more widely available assessments could be enhanced by capitalizing on technology as a means of delivering, scoring, managing, and storing assessments (see the chapter by Mislevy et al., 2003 and Pellegrino's commentary in this volume).

The proposed national initiative would establish assessments that could be used in evaluation and research on technology-supported learning and education more generally. Many of the assessments should themselves be technology-supported. To be useful and credible, the assessments would need to have demonstrated technical quality and endorsement from an unbiased, prestigious organization (such as the National Research Council).

CONCLUSION

In 1997 the Panel on Educational Technology of the President's Committee of Advisors on Science and Technology (PCAST) issued its report asserting that "a large-scale program of rigorous, systematic research on education in general and educational technology in particular will ultimately prove necessary to ensure both the efficiency and cost-effectiveness of technology use within our nation's schools" (p. 9). Given the fact that the current funding level for research on the learning impacts of technology-supported innovations (as described above) is less than a tenth of what the PCAST Panel viewed as necessary, any approximation to the PCAST recommendation would require a major change in the way the federal government thinks about and sponsors educational technology research. This synthesis is intended as a next step in conceptualizing the research needs, promising new approaches, and innovative research sponsorship arrangements to respond to that challenge.

Policy, Planning, and the Evaluation of Learning Technology

Nora Sabelli

Today's policymakers, educational practitioners, and the public have a strong interest in educational technologies. Educational research has been called on to provide evidence of their effectiveness. This confluence of interest and need for evidence along with new understandings of learning, cognition, and systemic reform combine to open new vistas for research and evaluation of education technologies. These real needs have resulted in calls for increases in funding for education technology research and in accountability for its learning outcomes. These in turn reflect an increase in public expectations about the impact of technology on student achievement. Thus researchers in education are being asked to demonstrate long-term causal links between technology and student achievement. Direct causal links are notoriously difficult to demonstrate within education studies, particularly when the intervention—in this case the application of technology—is so deeply embedded in the conditions of its deployment and pedagogical use.

There is, nevertheless, a need to plan for longer term studies of the use of technology in support of increased student achievement and a need for better understanding of the range of conditions under which such achievement is realized. Even more pronounced, in my opinion, is the need to design rigorous research on potentially ground-breaking uses of technology that are just emerging and have yet to achieve clear definition and a high rate of implementation.

I will discuss in this commentary the reasons why the question about the usefulness of technology in education keeps on being raised when many studies have shown when and how technology positively impacts learning. I am prompted to do so by the exciting prospects raised in this volume and in *Evaluating Educational Technology*. In particular, my analysis is consistent with Nick Smith's discussion of the critical importance of the questions posed as contrasted with the methods used (see Part I of this volume). I want to add to his points by discussing why we are only now in a position— methodologically and technologically—to move ahead and identify critical issues in evaluating a rapidly moving target such as learning technology.

The perspective I take is one arrived at after 10 years at the National Science Foundation supporting research at the intersection of technology, science, and education, and membership in a number of federal interagency committees coordinating activities in the same area. I have learned to see the limitations of depending on short-term answers to long-term questions, especially in the absence of an understanding of how these answers can help—or hinder—building a stronger base for long-term success.

My goal is not to analyze or review the chapters in *Evaluating Educational Technology* or the summaries and critiques in this volume. Rather, it is to point out the policy conditions under which these costly research studies may be undertaken and under which the results of such long-term evaluations would be considered. My perspective on policy has been influenced by research from other fields that focuses on complex social organizations, of which the educational system is but one instance. In particular, I have considerations of policy learning (May, 1999) and research from other fields such as resource management where the interplay between local uses and general knowledge is paramount (Holling, 1995).

These ideas form part of current thinking about adaptive management techniques derived from complex natural systems and are related to a deeper understanding of the role of social science research in policy learning (see, e.g., Flyvberg, 2001). As Holling (1995) puts it, "Therefore, the focus best suited for the natural science components is evolutionary, for economics and organizational theory is learning and innovation, and for polices is actively adaptive designs that yield understanding as much as they do product."

I take also, as a starting point, what Margaret Mead (1959) once said, "Nobody will live all his life in the world into which he is born and nobody will die in the world in which he worked in his maturity" (p. 34). As much as we recognize the truth of this statement in our lives outside of education, we know that within it, arguments about the need for and nature of desirable change go on unabated. These are not arguments about pedagogy, technology, or science, or even their impact on society, as much as they are arguments about the goals of education, more appropriately, the balance among the manifold goals that society asks education to serve.

ARE WE ASKING THE RIGHT QUESTION?

There can be no general answer to the question "Does technology work in education?" independent of the particular technology and of the nature of its adaptation, and appropriation to local conditions, capabilities, and goals. We know from extensive research that technology works in education in the same way that we know that books work in education: The right book, with the right teacher, with the right pedagogy, will produce positive effects, given the right assessment (Roschelle et al., 2000). What we do not know, nor is there any way we could know, is whether technology works under any and all circumstances. Technology, all by itself, is no silver bullet for solving education's problems. We do know of some technologies that, when well applied by average teachers, work well (even when measured by standardized tests, but also as indicated by other critical measures, such as lower dropout rates, higher attendance, and increased taking of rigorous courses). Since we know this, the question that is really being asked by local policymakers is rather "How would what we know works in some circumstances work best for us?"

It is not sufficient to know that something works; we need to understand *why* it works. Put in other words, educational implementation of innovations and of enhanced practices proven to work is dependent on fidelity to the original design. A high degree of fidelity is unattainable under the constantly evolving conditions of most classrooms. Only if we know why something works can we design implementations that allow teachers to both adapt the implementation to their needs and maintain fidelity to core design principles. Good evaluations must help practitioners understand what can and cannot be changed.

The expectation of causal attribution—what parts of the complex teaching and learning whole are attributable to technology—provides an additional problem. Success or failure is an outcome of the complicated partnership between parents, students, teachers, and society. Success or failure may have multiple causes, making the isolation of individual causal factors problematic. I believe that attribution poses a critical challenge, however, only if attribution is sought within individual implementations. By working at a more systemic level and analyzing results across implementations, we can make more credible causal inferences.

Although the question posed by policymakers and some writers appears as "Does technology work in education?" the truth of the matter is that we *are* putting technology in schools, students *are* learning with electronic resources now, and nobody is waiting for a formal answer to the question to plan their investments. The question as posed is meaningful when the interest lies in evaluating an isolated application, and is then equivalent to the information needed to choose between textbooks, for example. Useful as it is, this type of evaluation does not consider the more significant gains to be obtained by the use of technology across learning applications.

Evaluations of single applications are also misleading, in that they understate the costs and policy changes required by appropriate and effective uses of technology. The real questions being asked by policymakers and educators thinking of the outcome of their investments is "What are the effects that we can expect of using technology in education, so that we can determine the level at which to invest in it, and what do we need to do to maximize the return on our investment and gauge whether we are doing it well?" The same can be said for evaluating any school technology—installing a telephone or investing in a laboratory is of no use if those you want to communicate with do not also have a telephone, if you do not have time to use the phone or learn to use the laboratory, or do not have access to appropriate accounts or supplies.

We cannot forget also that education does not have a single goal; it has multiple ones, even if one considers student learning as the ultimate desirable and measurable outcome. An example that can tell us much about the importance of education goals and of the unavoidable law of unintended consequences is the national post-Sputnik push for science and mathematics education. In a very real sense, the push, the goal of which was to increase the number and quality of scientific professionals, was successful. Ask scientists of the appropriate age and they will have fond memories of the quality of the materials produced. But seen from a decades-long perspective, the post-Sputnik push left a legacy of the belief that "science is for the best and the brightest." This belief and the resulting tendency toward a "softer" curriculum for all other students, helped give rise to the deficiencies in science and mathematics education and the inadequate numbers of U.S. students training to become scientists that are still with us today, having outlasted the positive impacts of the excellent post-Sputnik instructional materials.

In retrospect, the goal should not have been to increase only the number and quality of scientific professionals but also to increase the quality of scientific education for professionals and others. The quality and number of professionals depends on the quality of and access to quality science and mathematics education for everyone. The first goal, we know in retrospect, is better addressed by integrating it with the second one, even though from the standpoint of individual students and their parents the goals may look quite different. The current systemic reform efforts, with their emphasis on quality education for all, take this position; though when it comes to challenging content, one can still hear doubts about the real meaning of "all students can learn." The lesson to be drawn is clear: Do not limit your response, evaluation, and actions to the short-term question at hand, but look beyond it to solve the real, larger, long-term problem.

When evaluating the impact of technologies on learning, arguments are often based on unstated assumptions about how the teaching and learning processes take place, about the assessment of learning, about the role of teachers and instruction, about how teachers learn to teach, and similar intermediary steps that define the interface of technology with learning in schools—in fact, the conditions for successful education. An unstated assumption is that things have always been and will always be as they are today. The images we all carry in our minds, by default and from attending school, are associated with the use of materials (textbooks, kits) for a single course or topic, and we look for evaluations of technology along the same lines (Confrey, Sabelli, & Sheingold, 2002). But how can we pose the real question regarding technology in education, given that technology is increasingly being used by schools in many different ways and is, in response, changing some of the assumptions we hold about the very nature of schooling?

WHAT SHOULD WE BE EVALUATING?

If one assumes that learning occurs by transmission from teacher to student, by students reading as directed and by following a series of more or less prescribed steps, both software and textbooks are equivalent, and we can evaluate them in the same way. We can use the same assessments to measure student learning with software or with a textbook, and we are justified in considering teacher knowledge and other variables the same in both cases. Many evaluations and meta-analytic studies conducted before 1990 take this stance.

One can also look for supportive technology uses (patient drill and practice, immediate feedback on errors as provided by electronic tutors, supplementary reading materials for special projects, and so on) that maintain the traditional learning assumptions. Since the underlying learning model has not changed when technology is used in these ways, we do not demand that evaluation and assessment measures change, and we may perhaps see a measurable shortening of the time-to-learn by more students as the benefit of technology.

If, on the other hand, the uses of technology of highest priority are ones expected to lead to higher order thinking, and to greater emphasis on individualized student-directed learning, we will need to consider additional measures of student learning, besides the traditional ones provided by standardized tests. Before deciding the learning outcomes that will be considered the mark of a technology's success, we need to be clear about the model of learning we are asking technology to support.

WHY EXISTING STUDIES ARE UNSATISFYING

One might expect that the positive impact found by meta-analytic studies of technology would be sufficient to convince policymakers of technology's usefulness. They are not sufficient, however, because the high costs associated with using technology force the question asked to be one of cost-benefit ratio rather than one of effect size per se. Answering this question is difficult because cost-benefit analyses are logically targeted to the aggregate uses of technology in schools, not to isolated uses.

In weighing the costs and benefits of providing technology to schools, we may want to consider the uses of technology that bring the school learning environment into closer connection with the world outside of school (i.e., facilitate teacher learning and access to outside-expert support and increase parent-teacher interaction).

Note that these views do not require that measures other than student achievement be used to evaluate technology; rather they require that "technology used by the school" be broadly defined in any study that purports to help policymakers and administrators judge (and plan for) the overall return on their investments, which could still be measured in large part by well-defined indexes of student achievement.

My experience with learning technology research at the National Science Foundation taught me that for technology to be effectively used as a tool in the hands of teachers and students, the following conditions must be in place:

- Access to technology supporting the acquisition and achievement of fluency with basic skills
- Technologies to support the development of higher level cognitive skills

- Technologies and allocation of class time in a way that allows students to work at their own pace until they master the material
- Technology supports for student independent work and communication skills in many disciplines
- Sufficient access time for students to learn

These points have implications for the limits of evaluations that use only standardized tests as student learning measures and make assessments only in separate disciplines, as well as of those conducted in schools with limited student access to technology.

For students to develop higher cognitive skills, the type of technology, the way that technology is implemented, the content and pedagogical preparedness of teachers, and the time available for teachers to become proficient become crucial variables.

Some of the most important effects on student learning are not visible at the end of a single short intervention but as the accumulation of learning experiences. Even if learning after a single intervention can be demonstrated, the desired return on the technology investment no doubt includes deeper changes in the ability of students to learn independently (e.g., enhanced retention of materials learned, the ability to learn more effectively in subsequent courses, the motivation to take more demanding science and mathematics courses, and the motivation to plan for postsecondary education).

For teachers to be able to support students in such higher cognitive learning tasks, alignment between access to technology, assessments, and teacher professional development has to be in place. This makes the policy and instructional environment of the school a variable that cannot be ignored. Policies, funding, and practice should be aligned in order to support learning outcomes.

The cost-benefit ratio for educational uses of technology does not depend on student learning outcomes achieved in a single discipline; it depends on outcomes achieved across disciplines and across years of schooling, and on the type of advanced knowledge and experience valued by the school. To achieve desired effects and to maximize return on investment, schools must provide the performance conditions that allow for achieving greater teacher and student learning outcomes. Longitudinal studies need to be performed that examine the intellectual and career growth of individual students and teachers, as well as the growth in achievement of cohorts of students moving through a school, as schools become better at providing good technology-enabled learning environments.

THE NEED FOR PROSPECTIVE RESEARCH

Evaluation often carries with it a connotation of studying the effects of what has already been done. But long-term evaluation and assessment research should look beyond the current limitations of technology, as discussed in several chapters in *Evaluating Educational Technology* and this companion volume. We must assume that the advanced systems that exist now only as prototypes in research laboratories will generate similar, widespread, low-cost systems in the future. Historically, the half-life of computers is about 3 to 5 years. If we base a research program on the study of currently available technology, and it takes several—let's say 5— years to conduct the longitudinal research, plus one or more years in advance of that to design the study, recruit participants, and develop instruments, plus several more years to make the research results known, we will clearly be developing research-based information that is obsolete. Instead, we should be helping to plan for a more effective implementation of the technologies of the future. The scope of a major learning technology research program must include new advanced systems and support bringing revolutionary computer and telecommunications developments and concepts into schools and classrooms in more effective ways.

Current and near-term uses of technology in schools are, for the most part, incremental in nature. If schools and environments were selected for a large-scale study on the basis of being representative of the rest of the system, a conservative bias from the perspective of future technology use, and hence near-term obsolescence, would be built in. As several chapters in *Evaluating Educational Technology* indicate, information technology will undoubtedly change some of the underlying assumptions of schooling and curriculum, as we know it. For example, if some projects currently funded by the National Science Foundation deliver on their promises, algebra and genetics may become topics of study for all students in elementary school, and calculus may become a middle school subject. Expert instructors will use networks to regularly supplement teachers in their role as classroom leaders. How will a long-term evaluation study incorporate these and other possible fundamental changes in curriculum and schooling as advanced technologies become widely implemented? Without the incorporation of such forward-looking practices, evaluations of technology will not be of much use in directing action; they will be retrospective rather than prospective. The design of a research and evaluation program should address this conundrum. Some of the chapters in the research volume start to do so, but none articulates a solution in any detail.

Any long-term evaluation that does not contemplate these, and similar, fundamental changes in technology (and associated changes in schooling) will produce answers 10 years from now that will be less useful than we have a right to expect—and may even delay advances in practice.

CONCLUSION

One of the barriers to conducting the types of studies needed has been the high level of funding they require. This may be less of a problem in the future as technology ceases to be considered a peripheral luxury by education policymakers. Once technology has become part of the fabric of everyday life and work outside of education, understanding its implications for education, both positive and negative, should become a higher priority for education funders and policymakers.

Understanding how to extract significant benefits from the investments made in technology's deployment is a different problem than understanding if a particular technology application works. The perspective that I think should be used when contemplating these evaluations is that of a world of practice as it may be 10 years from now—a perspective I take both because of my own experience and because of the very high rate of technological change. This experience leads me back to the focus chosen for the research chapters in *Evaluating Educational Technology,* the issue of research designs for assessing the long-term effects of educational technology on student learning. The chapters in *Evaluating Educational Technology* cover research and design approaches, emphasizing evaluation and assessment in a broad sense, but do not always deal with other aspects of education research, aspects that lie at the base of our knowledge of what is to be evaluated and that form part of the context that makes the enterprise possible now. This was a task better left to a policy epilogue such as this chapter.

There are many partial and very useful answers to the question of whether technology as an adjunct to current practice works, but I have argued that the nature of the problem is such that traditional measures of success do not necessarily provide the type of knowledge required by education administrators and policymakers for analyzing and maximizing the cost-benefit implications of their own local investments. Larger studies and random-assignment designs by themselves will not solve the problem of integrating technology's benefits for both traditional and advanced teaching and learning and for communications in support of education across all applications, subject areas, and grades.

Nor will such studies provide insights into what may be possible with tomorrow's technologies. As computers have become essential for representation, problem structuring, and analysis in many domains, they are extending human senses, intuition, and analytic capabilities, turning abstractions, like the laws of physics, into experiences. The national research agenda for learning technologies should do more than describe the impact of what has been done. It should provide guidance for the future, helping educators and policymakers negotiate this new terrain.

References

Adelman, N., Donnelly, M. B., Dove, T., Tiffany-Morales, J., Wayne, A., & Zucker, A. (2002, March). *Professional development and teachers' uses of technology. Subtask 5: Evaluation of key factors impacting the effective use of technology in schools* (Report to the U.S. Department of Education. SRI Project P10474). Arlington, VA: SRI International.

Bailey, J. (November, 2002). Discussant Comments for the Designs for Rigorous Evaluations of Learning. Technology Symposium for the American Evaluation Association. Arlington, VA.

Baker, E. L., & Herman, J. L. (2003). A distributed evaluation model. In G. D. Haertel & B. Means (Eds.), *Evaluating educational technology: Effective research designs for improving learning* (pp. 95–120). New York: Teachers College Press.

Becker, H. J., & Lovitts, B. E. (2003). A project-based approach to assessing technology. In G. D. Haertel & B. Means (Eds.), *Evaluating educational technology: Effective research designs for improving learning* (pp. 129–148). New York: Teachers College Press.

Becker, H.J., Ravitz, J.L., & Wong, Y.T. (1999). *Teacher and teacher-directed student use of computers in American schools.* Irvine, CA: Center for Information Technology and Organizations. University of California, Irvine.

Berliner, D. (2002). Educational research: The hardest science of all. *Educational Researcher, 31*(8), 18–20.

Chang, H., Henriquez, A., Honey, M., Light, D., Moeller, B., & Ross, N. (1998). *The Union City story: Education reform and technology-students' performance on standardized tests.* New York: Center for Children and Technology.

Coburn, C. (2001). Collective sensemaking about reading: How teachers mediate reading policy in their professional communities. *Educational Evaluation and Policy Analysis, 23*(2), 145–170.

Confrey, J., Sabelli, N., & Sheingold, K. (2002). A framework for quality in educational technology programs. *Educational Technology, 3*(42), 7–20.

Cook, T.D., Means, B., Haertel, G. D., & Michalchik, V. (2003). The case for randomized experiments. In G. D. Haertel & B. Means (Eds.), *Evaluating educational technology: Effective research designs for improving learning* (pp.15–37). New York: Teachers College Press.

Cronbach, L.J., & Snow, R.E. (1977). *Aptitude and instructional methods: A handbook for research on interaction.* New York: Irvington.

Cuban, L. (2000). Why are most teachers infrequent and restrained users of computers in their classrooms? In J. Woodward & L. Cuban (Eds.), *Technology, curriculum and professional development* (pp. 121–137). Thousand Oaks, CA: Corwin Press.

Culp, K.M., Honey, M., & Spielvogel, R. (2003). Achieving local relevance and broader influence. In G. D. Haertel & B. Means (Eds.), *Evaluating educational technology: Effective research designs for improving learning* (pp. 75–94). New York: Teachers College Press.

Doherty, K., & Abernathy, S. (1998). *Turning around low-performing schools: A guide for state and local leaders.* Washington, DC: U.S. Department of Education.

Education Commission of the States. (2001). *Comprehensive school reform: Progress and practices.* Available on-line: http://www.esc.org/.

Education Week. (2001, May). Technology counts 2001: The new divides. Available on-line: http://www.teachermagazine.org/sreports/tc01/index.cfm.

Erickson, F., & Guiterrez, K. (2002). Culture, rigor, and science in educational research. *Educational Researcher, 31*(8), 21–24.

Feuer, M. J., Towne, L., & Shavelson, R. J. (2002). Scientific culture and educational research. *Educational Researcher, 31*(8), 4–14.

Flyvberg, B. (2001). *Making social science matter: Why social inquiry fails and how it can succeed again.* Cambridge, UK: Cambridge University Press.

Grove Consultants International and the Institute for the Future. (2000). The educational technology horizon map and user guidebook. San Francisco: Author.

Haertel, G. D., & Means, B. (Eds.). (2003). *Evaluating educational technology: Effective research designs for improving learning.* New York: Teachers College Press.

Hedges, L. V., Konstantopoulos, S., & Thoreson, A. (2003). Studies of technology implementation and effects. In G. D. Haertel & B. Means (Eds.), *Evaluating educational technology: Effective research designs for improving learning* (pp. 187–204). New York: Teachers College Press.

Hendricks, M. (1982). Oral policy briefings. In N. L. Smith (Ed.), *Communications strategies in evaluation* (pp. 249–258). Beverly Hills, CA: Sage.

Hendricks M., Mangano M. F., & Moran, W. C. (Eds.) (1990). *Inspector generals: A new force in evaluation.* San Francisco: Jossey-Bass.

Holling, C. S. (1995). What barriers? What bridges? In L. H. Gunderson, C. S. Holling, & S. S. Light (Eds.), *Barriers and bridges to the renewal of ecosystems and institutions* (pp. 3–34). New York: Columbia University Press. Available on-line: http://www.tcd.ufl.edu/cdf/library/workpap/b-and-b/chapter1.html.

Honey, M., & Henriquez, A. (1996). *Union City interactive multimedia education trial: 1993–1995: Summary report.* New York: Center for Children and Technology.

Interagency Education Research Initiative (IERI).(2002). Prepared by the U.S. Department of Education, National Science Foundation, and National

Institute of Child Health and Human Development, Washington, D.C. Available on-line: http://www.ed.gov/offices/IES/ieri/ieri_rfa.doc.

Kaput, J., & Roschelle, J. (1998). The mathematics of change and variation from a millennial perspective: New content, new context. In C. Hoyles, C. Morgan, & G. Woodhouse (Eds.), *Rethinking the mathematics curriculum* (pp. 155–170). London: Falmer Press.

Kulik, C.C., & Kulik, J.A. (1991). Effectiveness of computer-based instruction: An updated analysis. *Computers in Human Behavior 7*(1), 75–94.

Lagemann, E. C. (2002). Usable knowledge in education. Chicago: Spencer Foundation. Available on-line: http://www.spencer.org/publications/index.htm.

Lesgold, A. (2003). Detecting technology's effects in complex school environments. In G. D. Haertel & B. Means (Eds.), *Evaluating educational technology: Effective research designs for improving learning* (pp. 33–74). New York: Teachers College Press.

Mann, D., Shakeshaft, C., Becker, J., & Kottkamp, R. (1999). *West Virginia story: Achievement gains from a statewide comprehensive instructional technology program.* Santa Monica, CA: Milken Family Foundation.

May, P. J. (1999). Fostering policy learning: A challenge to public administration. *International Review of Public Administration, 4,* 21–31.

Mead, M. (1959). Why is education obsolete? *Harvard Business Review, 36*(6), 22–36, 164–170.

Means, B., Haertel, G. D., & Moses, L. (2003). Evaluating the effects of learning technologies. In G. D. Haertel & B. Means (Eds.), *Evaluating educational technology: Effective research designs for improving learning* (pp. 1–14). New York: Teachers College Press.

Means, B., Wagner, M., Haertel, G. D., & Javitz, H.S. (2003). Studying the cumulative impacts of educational technology. In G. D. Haertel & B. Means (Eds.), *Evaluating educational technology: Effective research designs for improving learning* (pp. 230–256). New York: Teachers College Press.

Mislevy, R. J., Steinberg, L. S., Almond, R. G., Haertel, G. D., & Penuel, W. (2003). Improving educational assessment. In G. D. Haertel & B. Means (Eds.), *Evaluating educational technology: Effective research designs for improving learning* (pp. 149–180). New York: Teachers College Press.

Moses, L. (2000, February 25–26). *A larger role for randomized experiments.* Paper presented at the Invitational Meeting: Building a Foundation for a Decade of Rigorous Systematic Educational Technology Research, SRI International, Menlo Park, CA. (U.S. Department of Education grant R303U990001)

Murphy, R. F., Yarnall, L., Penuel, W., & Huang, J. (2003). *An educator's guide to evaluating claims about educational software.* Menlo Park, CA: SRI International Center for Technology in Learning. Available on-line: http://www.ncrel.org/tech/claims.

No Child Left Behind. (2001). Washington, DC: U.S. Department of Education. Available on-line: http://www.nclb.gov (April, 2003).

Olson, L., & Viadero, D. (2002). Law mandates scientific base for research.

Education Week, 21(20), 14–15.

Online Evaluation Resource Library. (2002). Center for Technology and Learning at SRI International, supported by National Science Foundation, Menlo Park, CA. Available on-line: http://oerl.sri.com (April, 2003).

Oppenheimer, T. (1997, July). The computer delusion. *The Atlantic Monthly,* 45–62.

President's Committee of Advisors on Science and Technology (PCAST), Panel on Educational Technology. (1997). *Report to the President on the use of technology to strengthen K–12 education in the United States.* Washington, DC: Author.

Public School Technology Survey 2001. (2001). Trenton, NJ: New Jersey Department of Education. Available on-line: www.state.nj.us/njded/techno/survey/results/.

Puma, M., Chaplin, D., & Pape, A. (2000). *E-rate and the digital divide: A preliminary analysis from the integrated studies of educational technology* (Report to the U.S. Department of Education). Washington, DC: Urban Institute. Available on-line: http://www.urban.org.

Research on Learning and Education (ROLE). (1999). Washington, DC: National Science Foundation. Available on-line: http://www.nsf.gov/pubs/2000/nsf0017/nsf0017.html.

Rodriguez, J. (2002, December 19). Free laptops not worth price to education. San Jose Mercury News, p. 1B.

Roschelle, J., Pea, R., Hoadley, C., Gordin, D., & Means, B. (2000). Changing how and what children learn in school with collaborative cognitive technologies. *The Future of Children, 10*(2), 76–101.

Rumberger, R. W. (2003). The advantages of longitudinal design. In G. D. Haertel & B. Means (Eds.), *Evaluating educational technology: Effective research designs for improving learning* (pp. 205–229). New York: Teachers College Press.

Scriven, M. (1991). *Evaluation thesaurus* (4th ed.). Newbury Park, CA: Sage.

Shymansky, J. A., Kyle, W. C., & Alport, J. M. (1983). The effects of new science curricula on student performance. *Journal of Research in Science Teaching, 20*(5), 387–404.

Simmons, W., & Resnick, L. (1993). Assessment as the catalyst of school reform. *Educational Leadership, 50*(5), 11–15.

Spillane, J.P., Reiser, B. J., & Reimer, T. (2002). Policy implementation and cognition: Reframing and refocusing implementation research. *Review of Educational Research, 72*(3), 387–431.

Stokes, D. E. (1997). *Pasteur's quadrant: Basic science and technological innovation.* Washington, DC: Brookings Institution Press.

Stoll, C. (1995). *Silicon snake oil: Second thoughts on the information highway.* New York: Doubleday.

U.S. Department of Education. (1998). *Catalog of school reform models* (1st edition). Washington, DC: Author.

U.S. Department of Education. (2002, April). New directions for program evaluation of the U.S. department of education. Available on-line: http://www.ed.gov/PressReleases/04-2002/evaluation.html

U.S. Department of Education, Institute of Education Sciences. (2002). What Works Clearinghouse (WWC). Available on-line: http://www.w-w-c.org/topicnom.html.

U.S. Department of Education, Office of Educational Technology. (1996). Getting America's students ready for the twenty-first century: Meeting the technology literacy challenge. Washington, DC: Author.

U.S. Department of Education, Office of Educational Technology. (2001). E-learning: Putting world-class education at the fingertips of all children. Washington, DC: Author.

Viadero, D. (2000). House plan would create research academy. *Education Week, 19*(43), 30.

About the Contributors

Geneva D. Haertel is a Senior Educational Researcher at the Center for Technology in Learning at SRI International. Her research has focused on influences on student learning, assessment, and evaluation of K–12 education programs. She has published over 40 articles on the conditions that promote student achievement. She has also contributed to the knowledge base on research designs and assessments used in studies of educational reform. In 1997, she co-edited *Psychology and Educational Practice;* in 1993, she co-authored the *Resource Handbook of Performance Assessment and Measurement;* and in 1991, she co-edited the *International Encyclopedia of Educational Evaluation.*

Valerie E. Lee is a Professor of Education at the University of Michigan and a faculty associate at the University's Institute for Social Research. She teaches courses in the Sociology of Education, Program Evaluation, and Quantitative Methods. Her research focuses on issues of equity in education, particularly characteristics of schools and classrooms that are associated with student learning and its equitable distribution. She has recently summarized a series of studies about secondary schools in *Restructuring High Schools for Equity and Excellence: What Works* (2001, Teacher's College Press). She has conducted research on young children, including *Inequality at the Starting Gate,* co-authored with David Burkam (Economic Policy Institute, 2002). She also co-authored, with Anthony Bryk and Peter Holland, *Catholic Schools and the Common Good* (1993).

Barbara Means directs the Center for Technology in Learning at SRI International, an independent nonprofit research organization based in Menlo Park, CA. Her research focuses on ways to foster students' learning of advanced skills and the changes in practice at the school and classroom levels associated with the introduction of technology-supported innovations. She has directed numerous research projects concerned with the design, implementation, and evaluation of technology-enhanced approaches to education reform. Her recent work includes case studies of technology use in urban high schools, published as *The Connected School.* Her earlier published works include the edited volumes *Technology and Education Reform* and *Teaching Advanced Skills to At-Risk Students.*

James W. Pellegrino is Distinguished Professor of Cognitive Psychology and Education at the University of Illinois at Chicago where he also serves as co-director of UIC's Center for the Study of Learning, Instruction, and Teacher Development. His research and development interests focus on children's and adults' thinking and learning, and the implications of cognitive research and theory for assessment and instructional practice. Much of his current work is focused on analyses of complex learning and instructional environments, including those incorporating powerful information technology tools, with the goal of better understanding the nature of student learning and the conditions that enhance deep understanding. He has served as head of several National Academy of Science/National Research Council study committees including the committee which issued the recent report *Knowing What Students Know: The Science and Design of Educational Assessment.* He is a lifetime National Associate of the National Academy of Sciences and a member of the Board on Testing and Assessment of the National Research Council. He has supervised several large-scale research and development projects funded by federal agencies and private foundations and has authored or co-authored over 200 books, chapters and journal articles in the areas of cognition, instruction and assessment.

Linda G. Roberts directed the U.S. Department of Education's Office of Educational Technology from its inception in September 1993 to January 2001, and served as the Secretary of Education's Senior Adviser on Technology. Previously at the U.S. Congress, Office of Technology Assessment, Roberts headed up that office's assessments of educational technology and authored three national reports: *Power On! New Tools for Teaching and Learning; Linking for Learning: A New Course for Education; and Adult Literacy and Technology: Tools for a Lifetime.* She is a former elementary school teacher and reading specialist, K–12 reading coordinator, university professor, and academic dean. Roberts now serves as senior adviser to several companies, foundations and government agencies, and is a member of the Board of Trustees of the Sesame Workshop and the Education Development Center and is a member of the boards of directors of Wireless Generation and Carnegie Learning.

Nora Sabelli co-directs (with Barbara Means) the Center for Technology and Learning at SRI International. Her professional research training was in computational chemistry, but her work since the early nineties focuses on the roles of research and technology in providing quality science, mathematics and technology education reflective of current scientific advances and technology trends. Dr. Sabelli joined the National Science Foundation in 1993 until her retirement in 2001. In 1998 she was on detail to the White House National Science and Technology Council, working at the Office of Science and Technology Policy on issues of research, technology, and education. Her NSF directorship included collaboration with the NSF-wide programs of Research on Learning and Education, Learning and Intelligent Systems and Research on Education, Policy and Practice Program. She was also for one year Senior Research Fellow at the University of Texas, Austin, working with the SYRCE. (Systemic Research Collaborative for Research in Education in Mathematics, Science and Technology).

Nick L. Smith is a Professor in the Instructional Design, Development, and Evaluation program of the School of Education at Syracuse University. His primary areas of interest include evaluation theory and the methodology of applied social science research and evaluation, having published over 100 articles and 8 edited volumes on related topics. Nick has served on numerous editorial boards, and is the 2004 president of the American Evaluation Association.

Julia Stapleton was with the New Jersey Department of Education for 16 years. As the director for the Office of Educational Technology, Julia coordinated numerous statewide programs related to technology infusion and evaluation practices. Under Julia's leadership, 21 county-based Educational Technology Training Centers were established, Distance Learning Network Aid increased to more than $55 million per year, the innovative Technology Fellowship: Mentoring and Modeling program was implemented, and 12 major competitive grant programs awarded more than $40 million to schools throughout the state. Assessment was a key component of all programs. Prior to joining the department, Julia was a teacher (Parsippany-Troy Hills and Hopatcong School Districts) and served as an educational technology consultant throughout New Jersey. Julia is currently the supervisor of grants for Elizabeth Public Schools, an urban school district with more than 20,000 students.

Index